LUXURY HOUSES

CITY

LUXURY HOUSES

CITY

edited by Cristina Paredes Benítez

teNeues

Editor and texts: Cristina Paredes Benítez

Art Director: Mireia Casanovas Soley

Layout: Nil Solà Serra

Translations: Enrique Góngora Padilla (English)
Marion Westerhoff (French)
Martin Fischer (German)
Donatella Talpo (Italian)

Produced by Loft Publications
www.loftpublications.com

Published by teNeues Publishing Group

teNeues Publishing Company
16 West 22nd Street, New York, NY 10010, USA
Tel.: 001-212-627-9090, Fax: 001-212-627-9511

teNeues Book Division
Kaistraße 18, 40221 Düsseldorf, Germany
Tel.: 0049-(0)211-994597-0, Fax: 0049-(0)211-994597-40

teNeues Publishing UK Ltd.
P.O. Box 402, West Byfleet, KT14 7ZF, Great Britain
Tel.: 0044-1932-403509, Fax: 0044-1932-403514

teNeues France S.A.R.L.
4, rue de Valence, 75005 Paris, France
Tel.: 0033-1-55 76 62 05, Fax: 0033-1-55 76 64 19

teNeues Iberica S.L.
Pso. Juan de la Encina 2–48, Urb. Club de Campo
28700 S.S.R.R., Madrid, Spain
Tel./Fax: 0034-91-65 95 876

www.teneues.com

ISBN-10:   3-8327-9062-4
ISBN-13:   978-3-8327-9062-2

Bibliographic information published by
Die Deutsche Bibliothek. Die Deutsche Bibliothek lists
this publication in the Deutsche Nationalbibliografie;
detailed bibliographic data is available in the Internet
at http://dnb.ddb.de.

Contents

Introduction

Luxury can be equated to quality, exclusivity and magnificence, among other terms, and take on different forms. It is widely accepted that luxury may refer to—and depend on—the most varied and different styles and ambiances. And although elegance and distinction may be subject to different readings, the distinguishing feature of genuine luxury, as opposed to soul-less opulence, is a certain degree of excellence and the quality of the materials and objects involved.

For centuries, cities have been the locus of cultural exchange and constant demographic dynamism; they are centers of business in which economic activity leads to large financial transactions. It is precisely in cities where we can find exclusive shops and most of the prestigious restaurants and innovative clubs, alongside various activities of all kinds. These are places in which we can easily come in contact with luxury.

In view of their fast pace of life, city dwellers are in need of comfortable and welcoming houses where they can rest, relax and unwind after a frantic day. Therefore, residences become spaces for exclusivity, personalized to meet the tastes of their owners and filled with objects that are in fact a symbol of economic status, as well as social and class standing. The houses feature magnificent decoration, antique or contemporary design furniture and works of art of different periods and styles.

The houses shown in this book are located in some of the most lively and attractive cities in the world: New York, Los Angeles and London, among others. The combination of different decorative styles is one of their most outstanding features. In the following pages you can solace with splendid examples of tradition and modernity at a time, and with interiors in which western and oriental decoration are integrated. All projects show sophisticated, attractive and sumptuous interiors that meet the needs of urban life, with traditional and classical styles presented alongside other more contemporary ones, thus showing the wide range of possibilities offered by the luxury market nowadays.

Einleitung

Luxus, das heißt auch Qualität, Exklusivität und Pracht. Aber Luxus gestaltet sich sehr unterschiedlich, je nachdem, auf welchen Stil und auf welche Wohnumwelt er sich bezieht. Eleganz und Ausgefallenheit können sehr unterschiedliche Formen annehmen, und was echten Luxus von großsprecherischer Fülle unterscheidet, ist eben eine gewisse Vortrefflichkeit und Qualität in der Auswahl der Materialien und Einrichtungsgegenstände.

Seit vielen Jahrhunderten sind die Städte aufgrund des ständigen Kommens und Gehens vieler Menschen Orte des kulturellen Austauschs, Wirtschafts- und Handelszentren, in denen große Mengen an Geld bewegt werden. In den Städten findet man daher die exklusiven Boutiquen, die meisten renommierten Restaurants und die neuesten Clubs und ein breitgefächertes Angebot aller Freizeitaktivitäten. Hier fällt es daher auch nicht schwer, echten Luxus zu finden.

Angesichts des schnelllebigen Rhythmus der Städte suchen ihre Bewohner komfortable, behagliche Wohnungen, in denen sie sich von der Hast des Tages erholen können. Die Wohnung wird zu einem exklusiven Bereich, den die Besitzer ihren persönlichen Vorlieben entsprechend einrichten und mit unzähligen Gegenständen anfüllen, die auf ein gehobenes Einkommen, soziales Prestige und einen auserlesenen Geschmack hindeuten. Man findet prachtvolle Dekorationen, Antiquitäten, und zeitgenössische Designerstücke und Kunstwerke aller Epochen und Stile.

In diesem Buch werden Wohnhäuser vorgestellt, die in einigen der attraktivsten und dynamischsten Städte der Welt liegen, darunter New York, Los Angeles und London. In vielen fällt die Kombination verschiedener Einrichtungsstile besonders ins Auge. Auf den nächsten Seiten finden Sie herausragende Beispiele für das Nebeneinander von Tradition und Moderne, Sie entdecken Interieurs, die östliche und westliche Dekorationen vereinen. Die Projekte stellen wohl durchdachte, attraktive und glanzvolle Innenräume vor, die sich den Erfordernissen des Lebens in der Stadt anpassen. Klassische und traditionelle Entwürfe stehen neben zeitgenössischen Vorschlägen und präsentieren einen breiten Fächer der Möglichkeiten, den der Luxus unserer Tage zu bieten hat.

Introduction

Le luxe, synonyme de qualité, exclusivité et magnificence, entre autres, peut se manifester de différentes façons. Il va sans dire que le terme de luxe est très relatif et qu'il peut se référer à des styles et des ambiances diverses. Si les interprétations de l'élégance et de la distinction peuvent être différentes, ce qui distingue le luxe authentique d'une opulence futile, c'est un certain grade d'excellence et de qualité dans les matériaux et les objets.

Depuis des siècles, les villes sont des lieux d'échange culturel qui connaissent une évolution démographique constante, centres de négoces et d'activités économiques mobilisant de grosses sommes d'argent. Ce sont précisément les villes qui accueillent les boutiques exclusives, la plupart des restaurants prestigieux et clubs innovants sans oublier un large éventail d'offre d'activités diverses. Ce sont des lieux où le luxe est omniprésent.

Le rythme de vie trépidant des villes fait que leurs habitants sont en quête de foyers confortables et accueillants où se reposer, se détendre et se déconnecter du rythme effréné du quotidien. Les résidences se convertissent donc en espaces très exclusifs, personnalisés pour répondre au goût des propriétaires et débordants d'objets qui sont en réalité des symboles révélateurs du niveau économique élevé, du prestige atteint et de la classe sociale. Ces demeures accueillent des décorations splendides, déclinant mobilier ancien, design contemporain, œuvres d'art d'époques et styles différents.

Les demeures réunies dans cet ouvrage sont situées au sein des plus attrayantes et vivantes villes du monde, à l'instar de New York, Los Angeles et Londres, pour ne citer qu'elles. Le mélange de divers styles décoratifs est un des éléments partagés par la plupart de ces résidences. Les pages suivantes offrent de splendides exemples de l'alliance entre tradition et modernité, d'intérieurs intégrant décoration occidentale et orientale. Les projets montrent tous ces intérieurs recherchés, attrayants et somptueux, qui tiennent compte des besoins de la vie citadine. Styles classiques, traditionnels et plus contemporains se côtoient pour montrer le large éventail de possibilités qu'offre de nos jours, le marché du luxe.

Introducción

El lujo, sinónimo de calidad, exclusividad y magnificencia, entre muchos otros, puede manifestarse de diferentes formas. Es de sobra sabido que el término lujoso es muy relativo y que puede referirse a estilos y ambientes distintos. Si bien la elegancia y la distinción ofrecen varias lecturas, lo que distingue al auténtico lujo de una opulencia vacía es un cierto grado de excelencia y calidad en los materiales y objetos.

Desde hace siglos, las ciudades son lugares de intercambio cultural que experimentan un constante movimiento demográfico, centros de negocios y de actividades económicas donde se mueven grandes sumas de dinero. Es precisamente en las ciudades donde se hallan exclusivas boutiques, prestigiosos restaurantes e innovadores clubes, y una amplia oferta de actividades de todo tipo. Son lugares donde el lujo puede encontrarse fácilmente.

El ritmo de vida trepidante de las ciudades hace que sus habitantes necesiten unos hogares confortables y acogedores donde descansar, relajarse y desconectar del frenético día a día. Las residencias se convierten, por tanto, en espacios de gran exclusividad, personalizados para adecuarse al gusto de los propietarios y repletos de objetos que son en realidad símbolos que denotan un alto nivel económico, prestigio social y clase. En ellas se pueden encontrar espléndidas decoraciones, mobiliario antiguo o de diseño contemporáneo y obras de arte de épocas y estilos diferentes.

Las viviendas recogidas en este libro están situadas en algunas de las ciudades más atrayentes y vitales del mundo, como Nueva York, Los Ángeles y Londres, entre otras. La combinación de estilos decorativos diferentes es uno de los elementos más destacables en muchas de ellas. En las páginas siguientes se puede disfrutar de espléndidos ejemplos de tradición y modernidad al mismo tiempo, y de interiores que integran decoración occidental y oriental. Los proyectos muestran todos ellos interiores sofisticados, atractivos y suntuosos, en los que se tienen en cuenta las necesidades de la vida en la ciudad. Estilos clásicos y tradicionales se presentan junto a otros más contemporáneos para mostrar el amplio abanico de posibilidades que ofrece el mercado del lujo en nuestros días.

Introduzione

Il lusso, sinonimo di qualità, esclusività e magnificenza, ed molti altri, può manifestarsi in varie forme. E' ben noto che il termine lusso è molto relativo e può riferirsi a distinti stili ed ambienti. Sebbene l'eleganza e la distinzione offrono varie letture, quello che distingue l'autentico lusso da una opulenza vuota è un certo grado d'eccellenza e di qualità nei materiali e negli oggetti.

Da secoli, le città sono luoghi di scambio culturale che vivono un costante movimento demografico, centro d'affari e di attività economiche in cui si muovono ingenti somme di denaro. E' proprio nelle città in cui si trovano boutique esclusive, la gran parte di ristoranti di prestigio e di club d'avanguardia, ed una vasta offerta d'attività di tutti i generi.

Il ritmo di vita trepidante delle città fa sì che gli abitanti abbiano bisogno di case confortevoli ed accoglienti in cui riposare, rilassarsi e staccare dal frenetico tran tran quotidiano. Le residenze si trasformano, dunque, in spazi di grande esclusività, personalizzati per adeguarsi al gusto dei proprietari e pieni d'oggetti che in realtà sono simboli che denotano un alto livello economico, prestigio sociale e classe. In queste case si possono trovare splendidi arredamenti, mobili antichi o di design contemporaneo ed opere d'arte di varie epoche e stili.

Le case raccolte in questo libro si trovano in alcune delle città più attraenti e vitali del mondo, come New York, Los Angeles e Londra, tra le altre. L'abbinamento di diversi stili d'arredamento è uno degli elementi più rilevanti in molte di loro. Nelle pagine che seguono si troveranno splendidi esempi di abbinamento di tradizione e modernità, e di interni che integrano arredamento occidentale ed orientale. I progetti indicano interni sofisticati, attraenti e sontuosi, in cui si tiene conto delle necessità della vita in città. Si presentano stili classici e tradizionali insieme ad altri più contemporanei per mostrare l'ampia gamma di possibilità che offre il mercato di lusso ai nostri giorni.

A Flat in Madrid

☐ This magnificent residence is located in an avenue in the center of Madrid. The rooms were all made to open outwards, thus enabling to improve light conditions and space, which was the architect's purpose in this refurbishment. The furniture was purchased along the years in antique shops and some of them were customized, as is the case of the solid oak wood doors. The wooden floors in the living room and the wood panels were the only elements that were preserved after being thoroughly restored. Both these elements confer the flat a classical style in harmony with the rest of the rooms. The bedroom features an antique and luxurious retable used as a bed headboard while travertine marble was used in the bathroom.

☐ Bei der Neugestaltung dieser Wohnung an einer großen Straße im Zentrum von Madrid wurde besonderer Wert darauf gelegt, dass in alle Räume Tageslicht fällt. Durch diese Öffnung nach außen gewann die Wohnung an Helligkeit und an Großzügigkeit. Viele der Möbel haben die Besitzer im Laufe der Jahre antiquarisch erworben, andere wurden nach Maß angefertigt, wie auch die massiven Eichenholztüren. Bei der durchgreifenden Renovierung sind nur der Holzboden des Wohnzimmers und das eingebaute Regal erhalten geblieben, deren klassischer Stil mit der übrigen Ausstattung harmoniert. Weitere elegante und luxuriöse Details sind das Retabel als Kopfende des Bettes und das Bad in Travertin.

☐ La rénovation de cette magnifique résidence située sur une avenue centrale de Madrid a consisté, entre autres, à transposer les pièces vers l'extérieur. Cette ouverture sur l'extérieur, s'est accompagnée d'un gain de luminosité et d'espace, objectifs principaux de l'architecte. Le mobilier a été chiné, au fil des années, chez des antiquaires ou réalisé sur mesures, à l'instar des portes en chêne massif. Seuls le parquet du salon et les boiseries ont été conservés après avoir été méticuleusement restaurés. Ces deux éléments confèrent un style classique à l'ensemble qui s'harmonise avec les autres pièces. D'autres détails élégants et luxueux sont représentés par un retable ancien utilisé comme tête de lit dans la chambre à coucher et le marbre travertin de la salle de bains.

☐ La reforma de esta magnífica residencia situada en una céntrica avenida de Madrid ha consistido, entre otras cosas, en hacer que las estancias fueran exteriores. Al abrirse al exterior, se ha ganado luminosidad y amplitud, principales objetivos de la arquitecta. El mobiliario ha sido adquirido a lo largo de los años en anticuarios o bien se ha realizado a medida, como las puertas de roble macizo. Tan sólo se han conservado, tras una meticulosa restauración, el suelo de madera del salón y una boiserie. Estos dos elementos confieren un estilo clásico que armoniza con el resto de las estancias. Otros detalles elegantes y lujosos son un retablo antiguo que actúa como cabecero en el dormitorio y el mármol travertino del baño.

☐ La ristrutturazione di questa magnifica residenza situata in un viale centrale di Madrid ha avuto lo scopo, tra le altre cose, di rendere le stanze esterne. Aprendole verso l'esterno, si è guadagnato luminosità e sensazione di spazio, principali obiettivi dell'architetto. I mobili sono stati comprati nel corso degli anni presso antiquari oppure realizzati su misura, come le porte di rovere massiccio. Dopo un meticoloso restauro, si è conservato unicamente il pavimento di legno del salone ed una "boiserie". Questi due elementi conferiscono uno stile classico che ben lega con il resto delle stanze. Altri dettagli eleganti e di lusso sono una pala d'altare antica che funge da testata della stanza da letto, ed il travertino del bagno.

Location: **Madrid, Spain**
Architect: **Andrea Klamar Marsans**
Photograph © **Montse Garriga**

Feature space: **Entrance hall**

12

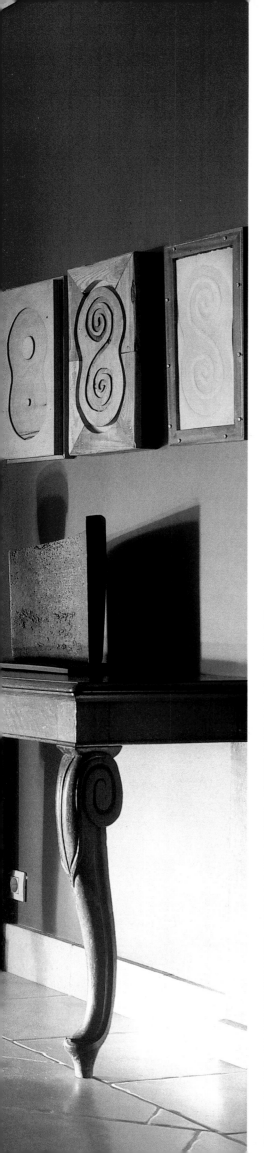

The entrance hall features an outstanding mix of elements and styles, from a Louis XV chair to an English console table, an African mask or a magnificent painting by the Belgian artist Yves Zurstrassen.

Die Diele zeichnet sich durch eine gelungene Stilmischung aus: ein Sessel im Louis XV.-Stil, eine englische Konsole, eine afrikanische Maske und ein großartiges Gemälde des belgischen Künstlers Yves Zurstrassen.

Le hall d'entrée se détache pour son mélange parfait d'éléments et de styles, depuis un fauteuil Luis XV à une console anglaise, en passant par un masque africain ou un magnifique cadre de l'artiste belge Yves Zurstrassen.

El recibidor destaca por una acertada mezcla de elementos y estilos, desde una butaca Luis XV hasta una consola inglesa, una máscara africana o un magnífico cuadro del artista belga Yves Zurstrassen.

L'ingresso colpisce per un abbinamento ben riuscito di elementi e stili, da una poltrona Luigi XV ad una mensola inglese, una maschera africana od un magnifico quadro dell'artista belga Yves Zurstrassen.

The bedroom is a large room with large windows that let the light come in through curtains and creates a relaxing and captivating atmosphere. The armchair and the foot rest make up an attractive and comfortable reading corner. As an outstanding feature, a piece of an antique wooden retable was used as a bed headboard.

Das geräumige Schlafzimmer erhält durch die Gardinen des großen Fensters ein angenehmes Licht, das eine entspannte, bezaubernde Atmosphäre schafft. Der Sessel und die Fußstütze laden zu angeregter Lektüre ein. Das ungewöhnliche Kopfende des Bettes wurde aus einem ehemaligen Retabel gefertigt.

La chambre à coucher est une grande salle dotée d'une large baie vitrée qui laisse passer la lumière au travers de rideaux, créant une atmosphère relaxante et fascinante. Le fauteuil et le repose-pied forment un coin de lecture attirant et confortable. L'appui-tête, créé à partir d'un fragment d'ancien retable, est un des éléments des plus remarquables.

El dormitorio es una gran sala con un amplio ventanal que deja pasar la luz a través de las cortinas y crea una atmósfera relajante y cautivadora. El sillón y el reposapiés forman un atractivo y confortable rincón de lectura; el cabecero, creado a partir de una pieza de un antiguo retablo, es uno de los elementos más destacados.

La stanza da letto è un'ampia sala dotata di una gran vetrata che lascia filtrare la luce attraverso le tende, creando in tal modo un'atmosfera rilassante e attraente. La poltrona ed il poggiapiedi creano un piacevolmente comodo angolo lettura; la testata, creata con una parte di un'antica pala d'altare, è uno degli elementi di rilievo.

Style and Elegance

☐ This luminous London residence has a magnificent and delicate decoration. A revival of a classical atmosphere is achieved by combining antique furniture, like the chests, with other contemporary style items, such as the armchairs upholstered in a zebra pattern. The white carpeted floor and the parquet in light tones create a luminous and graceful ambiance where the lavishness of small details stands out among the overall elegance. While the bedrooms and the entrance hall present a more classical aspect, the living room and the courtyard feature a more urban decoration.

☐ Dieses helle Wohnhaus in London weist eine großartige Einrichtung auf. Durch die Kombination von antiken Kommoden und anderen alten Möbeln mit Stücken zeitgenössischer Prägung, wie etwa den Sesseln mit Zebramuster, wird eine Atmosphäre des erneuerten Klassizismus heraufbeschworen. Die weiß ausgelegten Böden und das Parkett mit seinen hellen Farbtönen lassen die Räume leicht und luftig erscheinen und erzeugen eine elegante Atmosphäre, in der die vielfältigen Details gut zur Geltung kommen. Einige Räume, wie die Schlafzimmer oder die Eingangshalle, sind klassischer geprägt, während andere, wie der Salon oder der Innenhof, einer eher urbanen Linie folgen.

☐ Cette résidence londonienne, lumineuse, offre un décor à la fois subtil et magnifique. Le mélange de mobilier ancien, à l'instar des commodes, à d'autres meubles de style contemporain, comme les fauteuils aux motifs de zèbre, recrée une atmosphère de classicisme revisité. Les sols de moquette blanche et le parquet aux tons clairs créent une ambiance éthérée et lumineuse où l'on respire l'élégance et où l'on apprécie la richesse des détails. Quelques pièces, comme les chambres à coucher et l'entrée, sont plus classiques, tandis que d'autres, à l'instar du salon et du patio affichent une décoration plus citadine.

☐ Esta luminosa residencia londinense presenta una decoración delicada y magnífica. La combinación de mobiliario antiguo, como las cómodas, con otras piezas de estilo contemporáneo, como las butacas con estampado de cebra, recrea una atmósfera de clasicismo renovado. Los suelos de moqueta blanca y el parqué de tonos claros crean un ambiente grácil y luminoso, en el que se respira elegancia y se aprecia la riqueza de los detalles. Algunas estancias, como los dormitorios y el recibidor, son más clásicas, mientras que otras, como el salón y el patio, muestran una decoración más urbana.

☐ Questa luminosa residenza londinese presenta un arredamento delicato e magnifico. L'abbinamento di mobili antichi, come i cassettoni, ed altri pezzi di stile contemporaneo, come le poltrone con stampato zebra, ricrea un'atmosfera classica rinnovata. I pavimenti ricoperti di moquette bianca ed il parquet dai toni chiari creano un ambiente leggiadro e luminoso, in cui si respira eleganza e si apprezza la ricchezza dei dettagli. Alcuni ambienti, come le stanze da letto e l'ingresso, sono più classiche, mentre le altre, come il salone ed il cortile, presentano un arredamento più urbano.

Location: **London, United Kingdom**
Decorator: **Sarah Vanrenen**
Photograph © **Andreas von Einsiedel**

Feature space: **Entrance hall**

The stylish entrance hall area features a magnificent crystal door with a pointed arch that leads to a warm hall with fireplace in which a table and an antique vase are placed.

Die Eingangshalle ist sehr elegant gehalten: Eine prachtvolle Glastür mit Spitzbogen erschließt einen einladenden Raum mit einem Kamin und einem Tisch mit einer antiken Vase.

Le hall d'entrée est un espace très élégant : une somptueuse porte de verre, surmontée d'un arc en lancette, s'ouvre sur une pièce chaleureuse, dotée d'une cheminée et d'une table décorée d'une cruche ancienne.

El recibidor es un espacio muy elegante: una suntuosa puerta de cristal con un arco apuntado se abre a un cálido recibidor, con una chimenea y una mesa con un jarrón antiguo.

L'ingresso è uno spazio molto elegante: una sontuosa porta in vetro con arco a sesto acuto si apre su di un accogliente ingresso, con camino ed un tavolo con sopra un vaso antico.

The dining room is another of the eclectic rooms of this house. Some pieces of furniture and decoration objects are of classical style, like the chairs and the mirror, while others, like the lamp on the ceiling and the table, are more contemporary designs.

Das Esszimmer ist eklektisch eingerichtet. Einige Möbel und Dekorationsobjekte, wie die Stühle oder der Spiegel, sind klassisch zu nennen, während andere einer zeitgenössischen Optik folgen, wie die Deckenlampe oder der Tisch.

La salle à manger est une des pièces éclectiques de la résidence. Certains meubles et objets décoratifs sont classiques, comme les sièges et le miroir. D'autres, à l'instar de la lampe au plafond et la table, affichent un design très actuel.

El comedor es otra de las estancias eclécticas de la residencia. Algunos muebles y objetos decorativos son clásicos, como las sillas y el espejo; otros, como la lámpara de techo y la mesa, presentan un aspecto más actual.

La sala da pranzo è un altro degli ambienti eclettici della casa. Alcuni mobili ed oggetti decorativi sono classici, come le sedie e lo specchio; altri, come la lampada da tetto ed il tavolo, presentano un aspetto più attuale.

Quiet Atmosphere

☐ This luxury home was decorated with elegant furniture arranged in a classical and traditional manner. Simple lines and the interplay of contrasts are achieved by using light and dark tones that are the mark of nearly all of the decoration. This helps create delicate and simple atmospheres of great style, such as the one in the living room. The room is largely decorated in black and white, which contributes to give a sober and elegant look to the whole, in contrast with the warm moldings of the walls and the fireplace. Balance and simplicity are the defining features of its distinguished and highly stylish interiors.

☐ Dieses reich ausgestattete Haus vereint eine klassisch traditionelle Raumteilung mit elegantem Mobiliar. Aus dem Spiel der klaren Linien und den Kontrasten zwischen hellen und dunklen Farbtönen entsteht eine leichte, schlichte Einrichtung, deren Stilsicherheit sich z. B. im Salon zeigt. Die in diesem Raum vorherrschenden Farben schwarz und weiß wirken nüchtern und vornehm und stehen den warmen Tönen der Schmuckleisten an den Wänden und des Kamins gegenüber. In allen Räumen des Hauses herrscht ein ruhiges Gleichgewicht.

☐ La décoration de cette luxueuse demeure affiche un élégant mobilier et une distribution traditionnelle et classique. La simplicité des lignes et le jeu de contrastes entre les tons clairs et foncés, qui définissent presque toute la décoration de la maison, créent des ambiances délicates et sobres, très stylées, comme dans le salon. Les couleurs dominantes de cette pièce sont le blanc et le noir qui apportent une nuance sobre et élégante à l'ensemble, contrastant avec le côté chaleureux des moulures murales et de la cheminée. L'harmonie et le dépouillement définissent des intérieurs distingués et de grand style.

☐ La decoración de esta lujosa vivienda se ha resuelto con un elegante mobiliario y una distribución tradicional y clásica. La simplicidad de las líneas y el juego de contrastes entre tonos claros y oscuros, que definen casi toda la decoración de la casa, crean atmósferas delicadas y sencillas, con gran estilo, como el salón. Los colores principales de esta estancia son el blanco y el negro; éstos aportan un matiz sobrio y elegante al conjunto, que contrasta con la calidez de las molduras de las paredes y de la chimenea. El equilibrio y la sencillez definen unos interiores distinguidos y de gran estilo.

☐ L'arredamento di questa casa di lusso è stato risolto con mobili eleganti ed una distribuzione tradizionale e classica. La semplicità delle linee ed il gioco di contrasti tra toni chiari e scuri, che definiscono quasi tutto l'arredamento della casa, creano delle atmosfere delicate e semplici, con grande stile, come il salone. I colori principali di questo ambiente sono il bianco ed il nero che gli conferiscono un aspetto sobrio ed elegante, che contrasta con il calore delle modanature delle pareti e del camino. L'equilibrio e la semplicità definiscono gli interni eleganti e di grande stile.

Location: **London, United Kingdom**
Decorator: **Jasper Conran**
Photograph © **Andreas von Einsiedel**

Feature space: **Main bedroom**

Without doubt, the main bedroom is one of the most singular rooms of this house. The fireplace and the large windows create a delicately illuminated and friendly atmosphere. Two comfortable armchairs, antique closets, and two small bookcases complete the decoration of this room.

Das Schlafzimmer der Eigentümer ist zweifellos einer der ausgefallensten Räume des Hauses. Der Kamin und die hohen Fenster schaffen eine behagliche Atmosphäre und eine zarte Beleuchtung. Zwei bequeme Sessel, alte Schränke und zwei kleine Bücherregale ergänzen die Einrichtung.

Sans aucun doute, la chambre à coucher des maîtres est une des pièces les plus originales de la maison. La cheminée et les fenêtres hautes façonnent une atmosphère accueillante et un éclairage délicat. Deux confortables fauteuils, des armoires anciennes et deux petites bibliothèques complètent la décoration de la pièce.

Sin duda, el dormitorio principal es una de las estancias más singulares de la casa. La chimenea y las ventanas altas crean una atmósfera acogedora y una iluminación delicada. Dos confortables sillones, unos armarios antiguos y dos pequeñas librerías completan la decoración de la estancia.

Senza dubbio, la stanza da letto principale è uno degli ambienti più singolari della casa. Il camino e le finestre alte creano un'atmosfera accogliente ed un'illuminazione molto delicata. L'arredamento della stanza è completato da due comode poltrone, degli armadi antichi e due piccole librerie.

Some modern elements are perfectly integrated into the kitchen: the aluminum tops and the moldings in the ceiling are in perfect harmony. Likewise, some contemporary furniture is hidden behind the doors of an old larder.

Die modernen Elemente gliedern sich hervorragend in die Küche ein: die Arbeitsfläche aus Aluminium und die Stuckdecke leben einträchtig miteinander. Hinter der Tür des ehemaligen Speiseschranks verbergen sich weitere moderne Möbel.

Les éléments modernes s'intègrent à merveille à la cuisine : l'aluminium du plan de travail et les moulures du plafond cohabitent en parfaite harmonie. Certains meubles contemporains se dissimulent derrière les portes d'un ancien placard.

Los elementos modernos se integran perfectamente en la cocina: el aluminio en la superficie de trabajo y las molduras del techo conviven en perfecta armonía. También algunos muebles actuales se esconden tras las puertas de una antigua alacena.

In cucina gli elementi moderni si integrano perfettamente: l'alluminio del piano di lavoro e le modanature del tetto coesistono in perfetta armonia. Alcuni mobili attuali si nascondono dietro le porte di un antico armadio a muro.

An Art Dealer's House

□ This London house of great warmth belongs to an art dealer. The refined taste of its owner can be seen in the rooms decorated in classical style. The high-quality finish of its rooms and the luxury objects were carefully chosen to convey an air of luxury that enhances the building's splendor without being ostentatious. The lavishness and elegance of the house do not overshadow the warmth achieved in most of its rooms by using light colors that ensure a luminous and cozy ambiance. The garden is carefully looked after and provides a place for open-air rest and enjoyment in privacy.

□ Diese einladende Londoner Wohnung gehört einer Kunsthändlerin. Der feine Geschmack der Besitzerin spiegelt sich in der Einrichtung wider; klassische Dekoration, hervorragende Verarbeitung und ausgesuchte Stücke zeugen von einem zurückhaltenden Luxus, von einem überall spürbaren, aber niemals aufdringlichen Glanz. Pracht und Eleganz stehen nicht hinter Behaglichkeit zurück, denn in den meisten Räumen herrschen helle Farben vor und schaffen eine lichte, warme Atmosphäre. Der liebevoll gepflegte Garten bietet einen intimen Rückzugsort, an dem man angenehme Augenblicke der Entspannung unter freiem Himmel finden kann.

□ Cette demeure londonienne, accueillante, appartient à une marchande d'art. Le goût raffiné de la propriétaire se reflète à merveille sur son intérieur. Agencé dans un style classique, les finitions de grande qualité et les objets de décoration soigneusement choisis affichent un luxe mesuré qui laisse affleurer la splendeur de la demeure sans être ostentatoire. Somptuosité et élégance ne laissent pas la chaleur de côté, car la majorité des pièces sont dominées par les couleurs claires et les ambiances chaleureuses et lumineuses. Le jardin extérieur est entretenu avec un soin particulier, offrant un havre privé et agréable pour profiter des moments précieux de repos en plein air.

□ Esta acogedora vivienda londinense pertenece a una marchante de arte. El gusto refinado de la propietaria se refleja perfectamente en el interior; decorado con un estilo clásico, los acabados de gran calidad y los objetos de decoración cuidadosamente escogidos muestran un lujo comedido que deja aflorar el esplendor de la vivienda sin resultar ostentoso. Suntuosidad y elegancia no renuncian a la calidez, pues en la mayoría de las estancias predominan los colores claros así como las atmósferas cálidas y luminosas. El jardín exterior está cuidado con esmero y proporciona un rincón privado y agradable para disfrutar de agradables momentos de descanso al aire libre.

□ Quest'accogliente casa londinese appartiene ad una mercante d'arte. Il raffinato gusto della proprietaria si riflette perfettamente all'interno; arredamento in stile classico, rifiniture di grande qualità ed oggetti d'arredamento attentamente scelti mostrano un lusso garbato che lascia affiorare lo splendore della casa senza scadere nel pomposo. Sontuosità ed eleganza non appartano il calore, perché in gran parte degli ambienti predominano i colori chiari come pure le atmosfere calde e luminose. Il giardino esterno è curato nel minimo dettaglio ed offre un piacevole angolo privato per godersi gradevoli momenti di riposo all'aperto.

Location: **London, United Kingdom**
Decorator: **Barbara Ther**
Photograph © **Andreas von Einsiedel**

Feature space: **Dining room**

The living room also features a mix of warmth and elegance by which a sophisticated atmosphere is achieved. Bookcases with richly bound books and a magnificent antique mirror above the fireplace create a place of great style and lavishness.

Auch in diesem Salon erzeugen Wärme und Eleganz ein gehobenes Ambiente. Die Regale mit wertvollen Büchern und ein herrlicher alter Spiegel über dem Kamin tragen ebenfalls zur Vornehmheit des Raumes bei.

Le salon fait partie des pièces ou chaleur et élégance s'unissent pour créer une ambiance des plus exquises. Des étagères aux livres élégants et un superbe ancien miroir trônant sur la cheminée configurent un espace emprunt d'une élégance et richesse extrêmes.

El salón es otra de las estancias en las que calidez y elegancia se unen para crear un ambiente sofisticado. Estantes con elegantes libros y un magnífico espejo antiguo sobre la chimenea configuran un espacio de suma elegancia y riqueza.

Il salone è un altro degli ambienti ove si uniscono il calore e l'eleganza per creare un ambiente sofisticato. Mensole con eleganti libri ed un magnifico specchio antico sul camino creano uno spazio di estrema eleganza e ricchezza.

The owner's study is a comfortable and stylish room. Corinthian columns mark the entrance to a more personal room filled with books and objects from different origins. A cozy and intimate atmosphere was created by using warm colors.

Das Arbeitszimmer der Besitzerin ist bequem und elegant eingerichtet. Die korinthischen Säulen führen zu einem privaten Bereich mit vielen Büchern und Gegenständen unterschiedlichster Herkunft. Die warmen Farben vermitteln eine persönliche, warme Atmosphäre.

Le studio de la propriétaire est un lieu confortable et élégant. Des colonnes corinthiennes laisse le passage à une pièce plus personnelle, remplie de livres et d'objets d'origines diverses. Les couleurs chaudes créent une atmosphère personnelle et chaleureuse.

El estudio de la propietaria es un lugar confortable y elegante. Unas columnas corintias enmarcan la entrada a una estancia más personal, llena de libros y objetos de procedencia diversa. Los colores cálidos crean una atmósfera personal y acogedora.

Lo studio della proprietaria è un luogo comodo ed elegante. Delle colonne corinzie portano ad un ambiente più personale, pieno di libri ed oggetti di svariata provenienza. I colori caldi creano un'atmosfera personale molto avvolgente.

An Apartment in Mayfair

☐ This elegant house located in London's Mayfair features a neo-classic and French style decoration. The entrance hall, for instance, has a remarkable classical frieze. The house reveals the decorator's liking for color combinations, the unification of style in all the rooms and the creation of attractive interiors. The refurbishment included the opening of a skylight and the alteration of all the stairways. The best choice of materials was used, thus achieving first-quality finishes, as can be seen in the kitchen, in which three types of wood were used. The decoration achieves a certain feeling of joy of living surrounded by an air of traditional elegance throughout the house.

☐ Die Einrichtung dieses eleganten Apartments in Mayfair orientiert sich an französischen und klassizistischen Einflüssen; so findet sich im Vestibül ein klassizistischer Fries. In der Ausstattung spiegeln sich die Vorlieben der Innenarchitektin wider: Farben kombinieren, den Stil der einzelnen Räume einheitlich gestalten, attraktive Innenräume schaffen. Die Renovierung umfasste den Einbau eines Oberlichts und die Umgestaltung der Treppe. Man griff auf ausgesuchte Materialien zurück und achtete auf hervorragende Verarbeitung. Dies zeigt sich z. B. in der Küche, wo drei verschiedene Holzarten verwendet wurden. Dank der gelungenen Dekoration verspürt man im ganzen Haus „Joie de vivre" und traditionelle Eleganz.

☐ Dans cette élégante demeure du quartier de Mayfair, la décoration exalte de nettes influences françaises et néoclassiques, à l'instar du vestibule, avec une fantastique fresque classique. La demeure montre le talent de la décoratrice pour marier les couleurs, unifier le style des pièces et créer des intérieurs attrayants. La rénovation s'est attachée à la construction d'un velux et à la rénovation d'escaliers. Les meilleurs matériaux ont été employés pour obtenir des finitions de qualité maximale, à l'instar de la cuisine, où trois sortes de bois différents ont été employées. Grâce à la décoration, une ambiance de joie de vivre et d'élégance traditionnelle règne dans toute la maison.

☐ En esta elegante vivienda del barrio de Mayfair destaca una decoración con claras influencias francesas y neoclásicas; en el vestíbulo, por ejemplo, hay un fantástico friso clásico. La vivienda muestra el gusto de la decoradora por combinar colores, unificar el estilo de las estancias y crear atractivos interiores. La remodelación ha incluido la construcción de una claraboya y la reforma de las escaleras. Se han buscado los mejores materiales y se han conseguido acabados de máxima calidad, como puede apreciarse en la cocina, donde se han empleado hasta tres tipos de madera diferentes. La decoración logra hacer que se respire un ambiente de "joie de vivre" y de elegancia tradicional en toda la casa.

☐ In questa elegante casa del quartiere di Mayfair spicca un arredamento con chiare influenze francesi e neoclassiche; nel vestibolo, per esempio, vi è un fantastico fregio classico. La casa dimostra il gusto dell'arredatrice nell'abbinare colori, unificare lo stile degli ambienti e creare piacevoli interni. L'intervento ha incluso la costruzione di un lucernaio e la ristrutturazione delle scale. Sono stati scelti i migliori materiali ed ottenuto le rifiniture di massima qualità, come si può apprezzare in cucina, dove sono stati impiegati tre tipi diversi di legno. L'arredamento consente di respirare in tutta la casa un'atmosfera di "joie de vivre" e d'eleganza tradizionale.

Location: **London, United Kingdom**
Decorator: **Cecilia Neal**
Photograph © **Andrew Wood**

Feature space: **Crimson room**

The living room features a wooden-paneled bookcase and a sofa upholstered in crimson, all of which provides a warm atmosphere. The elegant and sophisticated look is achieved by combining some antique pieces with contemporary sofas and armchairs.

Das mit Holzpanelen verkleidete Regal und das karmesinrot bezogene Sofa geben diesem Salon eine behagliche Wärme. Antiquitäten werden mit modernen Sofas und Sesseln kombiniert, wodurch ein besonders elegantes und reizvolles Ambiente entsteht.

Au salon, une bibliothèque en lambris et un divan recouvert de rouge cramoisi confère une note chaleureuse. Les antiquités se conjuguent aux divans et fauteuils actuels dans un mélange qui confèrent à cette pièce élégance et raffinement extrêmes.

En el salón, una librería revestida con paneles de madera y un sofá tapizado en color rojo carmesí crean una atmósfera cálida. La combinación de antigüedades con sofás y sillones actuales confiere a esta estancia un aspecto extremadamente elegante y sofisticado.

Il calore nel salone è dato da una libreria rivestita con pannelli di legno ed un divano tappezzato in rosso intenso. L'abbinamento di pezzi antichi con divani e poltrone attuali conferisce all'ambiente un aspetto estremamente elegante e sofisticato.

The ivory tones of the room provide luminosity and create an ambiance that contrasts with the atmosphere of the library. The moldings of the ceiling and the walls alongside the use of busts and antique wall lights account for the great coherence in the classical decoration of this house.

Die Elfenbeintöne vermitteln Helligkeit und setzen diesen Raum von der Bibliothek ab. Die Einheitlichkeit der klassischen Ausstattung des Apartments kommt in den Stuckverzierungen an der Decke und den Wänden sowie den Büsten und den alten Wandlampen zum Ausdruck.

Les tons ivoire de la pièce subliment la luminosité et créent une ambiance différente de celle du salon et de la bibliothèque. Les moulures du plafond et des murs, voisinant avec les bustes et les appliques murales anciennes, exaltent l'harmonie du décor classique de l'habitation.

Los tonos marfil de la estancia aportan luminosidad y crean un ambiente distinto al del salón biblioteca. Las molduras del techo y las paredes, junto con la presencia de bustos y apliques de pared antiguos, muestran una gran cohesión en la decoración clásica de la vivienda.

I toni avorio della stanza danno luminosità, creando un ambiente diverso dal salone biblioteca. Le modanature del tetto e le pareti, insieme alla presenza di busti ed applique da parete antiche, dimostrano una gran coesione con l'arredamento classico della casa.

An Urban Resort

☐ All the rooms in this house are finely decorated in classical style, from the bathrooms to the study, which features comfortable armchairs, alongside other quality furniture and an accurate lighting. The main bedroom has a majestic bed with a canopy and salomonic columns. The armchair, the bench at the foot of the bed, the curtains and the rest of the furniture complete this profusely decorated room. The living rooms follow the same design as the bedroom, with rich upholstery that confers great warmth. Finally, a magnificent indoor pool gives a touch of distinction to the house.

☐ Die raffinierte Dekoration im klassischen Stil zeigt sich im gesamten Haus, von den Bädern bis zum Arbeitszimmer, wo sich bequeme Sessel, hochwertige Möbel und eine ausgeklügelte Beleuchtung finden. Das Schlafzimmer der Eigentümer wird von einem mächtigen Himmelbett mit gedrehten Säulen beherrscht. Der Sessel, die Bank am Fußende des Betts, die Vorhänge und die übrige Einrichtung sind reich verziert. Auch die Wohnräume sind in dieser Weise ausgestattet; die herrlichen Bezugsstoffe vermitteln Wärme und Behaglichkeit. Hervorzuheben ist schließlich das Hallenbad, ein unverkennbares Zeichen von Luxus.

☐ La décoration des pièces est raffinée et le style classique imprègne toute la maison, depuis les salles de bains jusqu'au studio, doté de fauteuils confortables, de mobilier de qualité et d'un éclairage bien étudié. La chambre à coucher des maîtres est présidée par un lit majestueux à baldaquin et colonnes torses. Le fauteuil, le banc aux pieds du lit, les rideaux et le reste du mobilier complètent cette pièce dotée d'une profusion de décoration. Les salons suivent la même ligne que la chambre à coucher, avec la richesse de leurs tapisseries qui rendent l'ensemble chaleureux. Enfin, il convient de signaler la magnifique piscine intérieure qui confère à la maison une touche de distinction.

☐ La decoración de las estancias es refinada y el estilo clásico impregna toda la casa, desde los baños hasta el estudio, donde se encuentran cómodas butacas, mobiliario de calidad y una estudiada iluminación. El dormitorio principal está presidido por una majestuosa cama con dosel y columnas salomónicas. La butaca, el banco a los pies de la cama, las cortinas y el resto del mobiliario completan esta estancia profusamente decorada. Los salones siguen la misma línea del dormitorio, con ricas tapicerías que aportan calidez al conjunto. Finalmente, cabe destacar la magnífica piscina interior, que aporta un toque de distinción a la casa.

☐ L'arredamento degli ambienti è raffinato e lo stile classico è presente in tutta la casa, dai bagni sino allo studio, ove si trovano comode poltrone, mobili di qualità ed una illuminazione ben studiata. La stanza da letto principale è presieduta da un maestoso letto con baldacchino e colonne salomoniche. La poltrona, la panca ai piedi del letto, le tende ed il resto dei mobili completano questa stanza profusamente arredata. I saloni seguono la stessa linea della stanza da letto, con ricche tappezzerie che conferiscono calore. Infine, da evidenziare la magnifica piscina coperta, che da un tocco di distinzione alla casa.

Location: **London, United Kingdom**
Architect: **Weldon Washle**
Photograph © **Jonathan Moore**

Feature space: **Indoor pool**

The indoor pool emphasizes the distinction of this house: the luxurious design of the room, as well as the oval shapes and the materials employed as covering, which create reminiscences of the classical thermal baths of antiquity.

Das Schwimmbad verleiht dem Haus eine besondere Klasse: Die luxuriöse Gestaltung des Saales, die ovalen Formen und die zur Auskleidung verwendeten wertvollen Materialien lassen an die Thermen und Bäder der klassischen Antike denken.

La piscine intérieure souligne la classe indéniable de la demeure : le design luxueux de la salle, les formes ovales et les matériaux employés pour les revêtements évoquent les thermes et les bains de l'antiquité classique.

La piscina interior subraya la indiscutible clase de la vivienda: el lujoso diseño de la sala, las formas ovaladas y los materiales empleados como revestimiento evocan las termas y baños de la antigüedad clásica.

La piscina coperta evidenzia l'indiscutibile classe della casa: il lussuoso design della sala, le forme ovali ed i materiali da rivestimento scelti evocano le terme, i bagni dell'antichità classica.

The bedroom is a special room featuring an impressive bed with a carved and gilded canopy and four salomonic columns. The air of magnificence of this room is emphasized by the rich materials and the upholstery employed.

Das Schlafzimmer ist ein einzigartiger Raum mit einem eindrucksvollen, geschnitzten und vergoldeten Himmelbett mit vier gedrehten Säulen. Der prunkvolle Eindruck wird von den verwendeten prächtigen Stoffen und Polsterungen noch verstärkt.

La chambre à coucher, forte de son impressionnant lit à baldaquin, travaillé et tout en dorures, avec ses quatre colonnes torses, est une pièce qui ne manque pas d'originalité. La splendeur qui émane de cet espace est sublimée par les toiles et tapisseries précieuses.

El dormitorio es una estancia singular, con una impresionante cama con dosel, labrado y dorado, y cuatro columnas salomónicas. La suntuosidad que se respira en este espacio se acentúa con las ricas telas y tapicerías.

La stanza da letto è un luogo singolare, con un impressionante letto a baldacchino, lavorato e dorato, e quattro colonne salomoniche. La sontuosità che si respira in questo spazio è accentuata dalle ricche tele e dalla tappezzeria.

Magnificent and Exotic

☐ A distinguished colonial look with touches of exoticism is the mark of this stately residence located in the capital of Indonesia. The rooms are decorated to enjoy various elements such as vases, old chests, wooden carvings and many other objects that make up an atmosphere designed by the owner with careful attention to sophistication. The exquisite furniture provides a touch of magnificence to the house. The transit areas that are sometimes overlooked here become great examples of good taste and richness. As can be seen in the study, the oriental touch in the decoration is perfectly integrated with the colonial style furniture to achieve a perfect balance.

☐ Dieses herrliche Haus in der Hauptstadt von Indonesien ist von exotischen Reminiszenzen mit einem kolonialen Touch erfüllt. Die Ausstattung der einzelnen Räume umfasst eine ganze Reihe dekorativer Objekte: Krüge, alte Truhen, Holzschnitzereien und vieles mehr tragen zu dem vom Eigentümer beabsichtigten gepflegten Gesamtbild eines repräsentativen Heims ebenso bei wie die ausgesuchten Möbel. Die oftmals vernachlässigten Übergangsbereiche zeugen in diesem Fall von Reichtum und einem exzellenten Geschmack. Im Arbeitszimmer wird deutlich, wie gekonnt sich die fernöstlichen Akzente in vollkommener Ausgewogenheit mit dem Mobiliar im Kolonialstil verbinden.

☐ Un air colonial distingué et des notes d'exotisme définissent cette majestueuse résidence située dans la capitale indonésienne. La décoration des pièces permet de profiter d'une foule d'éléments décoratifs : jarres, malles anciennes, sculptures en bois et autres, mettent en scène une atmosphère conçue avec soin et recherche par son propriétaire. Le mobilier est une merveille qui confère à la résidence toute sa somptuosité. Les zones de passage, parfois oubliées, sont ici des modèles splendides de goût et de richesse. Comme dans le studio, les touches orientales de la décoration s'intègrent à merveille au mobilier de style colonial, s'unissant dans une parfaite harmonie.

☐ Un distinguido aire colonial y notas de exotismo definen esta majestuosa residencia situada en la capital de Indonesia. La decoración de las estancias permite disfrutar de multitud de elementos decorativos: jarrones, baúles antiguos, tallas de madera y un largo etcétera componen una atmósfera diseñada con esmero y sofisticación por su propietario. El mobiliario es exquisito y aporta suntuosidad a la residencia. Las zonas de paso, en ocasiones olvidadas, son aquí espléndidos ejemplos de gusto y riqueza. Tal como se aprecia en el estudio, los toques orientales de la decoración se integran perfectamente en el mobiliario de estilo colonial y consiguen un perfecto equilibrio.

☐ Un'elegante aria coloniale e note d'esotismo definiscono questa maestosa residenza situata nella capitale indonesiana. L'arredamento degli ambienti consente di godersi tantissimi elementi decorativi: vasi, bauli antichi, statue di legno ed un lungo eccetera compongono un'atmosfera studiata con attenzione e sofisticazione dal suo proprietario. I mobili sono bellissimi e conferiscono sontuosità alla residenza. Le zone di passaggio, a volte dimenticate, sono qui degli splendidi esempi di gusto e ricchezza. Come si può vedere nello studio, i tocchi orientali dell'arredamento si integrano perfettamente nei mobili di stile coloniale ottenendo un perfetto equilibrio.

Location: **Jakarta, Indonesia**
Decorator: **The Owner**
Photograph © **Reto Guntli / Zapaimages**

Feature space: **Bedroom**

Wooden tones are used in the study alongside some ceramics pots to create a warm atmosphere. The mix of colonial style and traditional Indonesian decorative elements emphasizes the friendly ambiance of this room.

Holztöne und eine Reihe von Keramiken verleihen dem Arbeitszimmer eine warme Atmosphäre, die durch die Kombination des Kolonialstils mit traditionellen indonesischen Stücken noch unterstrichen wird.

Dans le studio, les tons du bois et des pièces de céramique se détachent pour créer une atmosphère chaleureuse. Le mélange de style colonial et d'éléments de décoration traditionnelle venant d'Indonésie exalte l'ambiance accueillante.

Destacan en el estudio los tonos de la madera y de las piezas de cerámica que se combinan para crear una atmósfera cálida. La mezcla de estilo colonial con elementos de la decoración tradicional de Indonesia acentúa el ambiente acogedor.

Spiccano lo studio in toni legno ed i pezzi di ceramica abbinati in modo da conferire calore all'ambiente. L'abbinamento di stile coloniale con elementi d'arredamento tradizionale indonesiano rende ancor di più accogliente l'ambiente.

The main bedroom again features a well-achieved fusion of styles. The wooden panels that cover the walls provide warmth and a feeling of comfort to this elegant and refined room filled with a number of small exotic objects.

Auch das Schlafzimmer des Besitzers zeigt eine gelungene Verschmelzung der Stile. Die hölzerne Wandverkleidung vermittelt einem in diesem eleganten, feinsinnig gestalteten Raum voller exotischer Details ein angenehmes Gefühl von Behaglichkeit.

La chambre à coucher des maîtres montre une parfaite fusion des styles. Les lambris des murs apportent chaleur et une sensation de confort à une pièce élégante et délicate, débordante de petits détails exotiques.

El dormitorio principal muestra nuevamente una acertada fusión de estilos. La madera que recubre las paredes otorga calidez y sensación de confort a una estancia elegante y delicada, llena de pequeños detalles exóticos.

La stanza da letto principale mostra di nuovo un'ottima fusione di stili. Il legno che copre le pareti da calore e sensazione di comodità ad un ambiente elegante e delicato, zeppo di piccoli dettagli esotici.

The inner courtyard is a space for enjoyment in the open air. A sofa with soft cushions, some old cases and umbrellas make up a place where time seems to be stopped, and which invites us to dream.

Im Innenhof kann man ruhige Stunden unter freiem Himmel verbringen. Hier scheint die Zeit still zu stehen: Ein Sofa mit bequemen Kissen, alte Koffer und einige Sonnenschirme laden zum Träumen ein.

Le patio intérieur est un espace où passer des instants agréables en plein air. Un divan doté de coussins confortables, des anciennes malles et des ombrelles recréent un espace où le temps semble s'arrêter, laissant place au rêve.

El patio interior es un espacio donde pasar momentos agradables al aire libre. Un sofá con confortables cojines, unas maletas antiguas y unas sombrillas recrean un espacio en que parece posible detener el tiempo y soñar.

Il cortile interno è uno spazio in cui trascorrere momenti gradevoli all'aperto. Un divano con comodi cuscini, delle valigie antiche e degli ombrelloni che ricreano uno spazio in cui sembra possibile fermare il tempo e sognare.

A House in New York

☐ This house is located in Manhattan and it was built in 1918; it became an apartment building in 1940 and, later on, it was finally recovered by its current owners. The residence was refurbished to respect its owners' desire for privacy while also becoming the place to hold a fantastic art collection, which required the installation of the environmental control and lighting systems that are used in museums. The house is laid out around two courtyards and a magnificent stairway that ascends gradually from one of them. The paintings that are hanging on the walls provide a touch of elegance and sophistication. All details were carefully looked after: the library, the dining room and the bathroom all present an absolutely perfect finish.

☐ Dieses in Manhattan gelegene Wohnhaus wurde 1918 errichtet, 1940 in ein Apartmenthaus umgewandelt und kürzlich von seinen jetzigen Eigentümern wieder der ursprünglichen Nutzung zugeführt. Das Gebäude sollte dem Bedürfnis seiner Besitzer nach Privatsphäre entsprechen und zugleich ihre sagenhafte Kunstsammlung beherbergen. Deshalb wurden Luftbefeuchter und Beleuchtungssysteme wie in einem Museum eingebaut. Das Haus ist um zwei Innenhöfe herum angelegt, in dem einen befindet sich eine originelle, sanft ansteigende Treppe. Die Gemälde an den Wänden verleihen der Wohnung einen kultivierten Gesamteindruck. Es wurde auf alle Einzelheiten geachtet; die Verarbeitung der Bücherregale ist ebenso perfekt wie die des Esszimmers und der Badezimmereinrichtung.

☐ Cette maison, située à Manhattan et construite en 1918, a été réhabilitée en 1940 en un immeuble d'appartements, pour être à nouveau restaurée par les propriétaires actuels. La résidence devant préserver le désir d'intimité des maîtres et héberger une collection d'art fantastique, a été dotée d'un système de contrôle d'ambiance et d'éclairage à l'image de celui des musées. La maison s'articule autour de deux patios dont l'un d'eux est pourvu d'un magnifique escalier latéral, en pente douce. Les cadres, accrochés aux murs, montrant un souci du détail extraordinaire, apportent une touche recherchée et élégante. La bibliothèque comme la salle à manger et la salle de bains affichent des finitions d'une perfection absolue.

☐ Esta casa, situada en Manhattan y construida en 1918, se transformó en un edificio de apartamentos en 1940 y fue recuperada de nuevo para los actuales propietarios. La residencia debía mantener el deseo de privacidad de los dueños y además ubicar una fantástica colección de arte, por lo que se instalaron unos sistemas de control ambiental y de luz como en los museos. La casa se articula alrededor de dos patios y junto a uno de ellos hay una magnífica escalera de suave pendiente. De las paredes cuelgan cuadros, que aportan un toque de sofisticación y elegancia, y se han cuidado al máximo todos los detalles; tanto la librería como el comedor y el baño presentan unos acabados absolutamente perfectos.

☐ Questa casa, situata a Manhattan costruita nel 1918, è stata trasformata in edificio d'appartamenti nel 1940, per poi essere nuovamente recuperata dagli attuali proprietari. La residenza doveva mantenere la voglia di privacy dei proprietari oltre ad accogliere una fantastica collezione d'arte, cosa che ha richiesto l'installazione di sistemi di controllo degli ambienti e della luce come nei musei. La casa si svolge intorno a due cortili, e vicino ad uno dei due vi è una magnifica scala con una leggera pendenza. Le pareti rivestite da quadri, conferiscono un tocco di sofisticazione ed eleganza, e qui ogni minimo dettaglio è stato curato al massimo; tanto la libreria quanto la sala da pranzo ed il bagno sono dotate di rifiniture assolutamente perfette.

Location: **New York, United States**
Architect: **Peter Rose**
Photograph © **Michael Moran**

Feature space: **Stairway**

The stairway is one of the most significant features of the refurbishment of this building: fine lines and a contrast of black and white. The magnificent works of art that are arranged on the walls create an atmosphere comparable to that of the best museums of the world.

Das Treppenhaus ist eines der charakteristischen Elemente der Renovierung: klare Linienführung und Schwarz-weiß-Kontrast. Die an den Wänden hängenden Kunstwerke erzeugen eine Atmosphäre wie in den namhaften Museen dieser Welt.

L'escalier est un des éléments les plus significatifs de la restauration de l'édifice : lignes épurées et contraste noir et blanc. Les magnifiques œuvres d'art accrochées aux murs créent une atmosphère comparable aux meilleurs musées du monde.

La escalera es uno de los elementos más significativos de la rehabilitación del edificio: líneas depuradas y contraste entre el blanco y el negro. Las magníficas obras de arte dispuestas en las paredes crean una atmósfera equiparable a la de los mejores museos del mundo.

La scala è uno degli elementi più rilevanti della ristrutturazione dell'edificio: linee depurate ed un contrasto di bianco e nero. Le magnifiche opere d'arte appese alle pareti creano un'atmosfera simile a quella dei migliori musei del mondo.

The large dining room has a sophisticated and elegant look. The large glass doors let the light flow in and lead to an inner courtyard.

Das Esszimmer ist ein großer Saal anspruchsvoller Eleganz. Prächtige Glastüren lassen reichlich Licht ein und öffnen den Raum zu einem Innenhof hin.

La salle à manger est une salle aux grandes dimensions qui affiche une esthétique sophistiquée et élégante. De grandes portes de verre, permettent à la lumière d'entrée en abondance, s'ouvrent sur un patio intérieur.

El comedor es una sala de grandes dimensiones que mantiene una estética sofisticada y elegante. Unas grandes puertas de cristal permiten la entrada de luz abundante y se abren a un patio interior.

La sala da pranzo è un ambiente di grandi dimensioni con un'estetica sofisticata ed elegante. Delle grandi porte di vetro lasciano passare molta luce, e si aprono su di un cortile interno.

Classical Elegance

☐ Elegance and liveliness are the main features of this magnificent residence located in Switzerland. Large chambers with splendid large windows provide luminosity and the decoration presents classical elements that also combine different styles of furniture with cheerful touches of color. The final result is a modern and original house with a lively and welcoming atmosphere. The combination of different floor materials also contributes to enhance the beauty of this attractive residence. Each of its rooms has a character of its own, with the main bedroom, the kitchen and the entrance hall as some clear examples of the singularity and distinction of the decoration.

☐ Diese prächtige Wohnung in der Schweiz offenbart vornehme Vitalität. Die großzügigen Fensterflächen schenken den weiten Räumen reichlich Licht. Die Einrichtung vereint klassische Elemente mit Stücken unterschiedlicher Stile, und durch die fröhlichen Farbakzente erhält die auf originelle Weise moderne Wohnung eine lebendige, gemütliche Atmosphäre. Die wechselnde Gestaltung der Fußböden erhöht den Reiz dieses Heims. Jedes Zimmer hat seinen eigenen Charakter; das Schlafzimmer, die Küche oder das Vestibül mögen als Beispiele für diese betont eigenwillige Dekoration stehen.

☐ Elegance et vitalité définissent cette somptueuse résidence en Suisse. Les grandes salles et les splendides baies vitrées apportent luminosité. La décoration présente des éléments classiques, même si elle est ponctuée de styles et pièces de mobilier variés, avec des touches de couleurs vives, qui configurent une demeure moderne et originale à l'atmosphère gaie et accueillante. Le mélange des sols, également différents, exalte aussi le charme de la résidence. Chaque pièce a son caractère propre et la chambre à coucher des maîtres, la cuisine et le vestibule, entre autres, sont un exemple de ce cette décoration originale et distinguée.

☐ Elegancia y vitalidad definen esta suntuosa residencia en Suiza. Las amplias salas y los espléndidos ventanales aportan luminosidad, y la decoración presenta elementos clásicos, aunque muestra estilos y piezas de mobiliario variados, con alegres toques de color, que configuran una vivienda moderna y original con una atmósfera viva y acogedora. La combinación de suelos distintos también contribuye a aumentar el atractivo de la residencia. Cada estancia tiene un carácter propio, y el dormitorio principal, la cocina y el vestíbulo, por ejemplo, son una clara muestra de esta singular y distinguida decoración.

☐ Eleganza e vitalità definiscono questa sontuosa residenza in Svizzere. Le grandi sale e gli splendidi finestroni danno luminosità, e l'arredamento presenta elementi classici, pur mostrando stili e mobili vari, con allegri tocchi di colore, che danno carattere ad una casa moderna ed originale dotata di un'atmosfera viva ed accogliente. L'abbinamento di diversi pavimenti contribuisce ad aumentare la bellezza della residenza. Ogni ambiente ha un carattere proprio, e la stanza da letto principale, la cucina ed il vestibolo, per esempio, sono una chiara dimostrazione della singolarità elegante di questo arredamento.

Location: **Zurich, Switzerland**

Decorator: **Sue Rohrer**

Photograph © **Bruno Helbling / Zapaimages**

Feature space: **Fireplace chamber**

The main room is laid out around a great fireplace. Paintings and drawings are displayed on the walls, which are painted bright red; the television screen and several living areas are also arranged in this original and stylish room which is undoubtedly the forte of this residence.

Das große Wohnzimmer wird vom Kamin beherrscht. An den leuchtend rot gestrichenen Wänden hängen Gemälde und Zeichnungen. Außer der Fernsehecke wurden hier noch andere Aufenthaltsbereiche eingerichtet. Dieser originelle und stilvolle Raum ist unbestreitbar der Mittelpunkt des Hauses.

La salle principale s'articule autour d'une grande cheminée. Cadres et dessins sont accrochés sur les murs, peints en rouge vif. Il y a aussi un coin télévision et différentes zones de salon. Originale et stylée, c'est sans aucun doute la pièce phare de cette résidence.

La sala principal se articula en torno a una gran chimenea. En las paredes, pintadas de un rojo brillante, hay cuadros y dibujos colgados; también se ha colocado una televisión y se han dispuesto diferentes zonas de estar. Original y con estilo, es sin duda la estancia protagonista de esta residencia.

La sala principale si svolge intorno ad un gran camino. Sulle pareti, pitturate in rosso brillante, vi sono quadri e disegni appesi; vi è anche una televisione e varie zone di soggiorno. Originale e con stile, è, senza dubbio, l'ambiente protagonista di questa residenza.

The study has a historical atmosphere. The table, the bookcases and the cases are all very well-preserved antique pieces. The globes and the old books in the bookcase put an emphasis on the stateliness of the atmosphere.

Im Arbeitszimmer spürt man den Atem der Geschichte. Der Schreibtisch, der Bücherschrank und die Koffer sind gut erhaltene antike Stücke, die mit den Globen und den wertvollen alten Büchern gut harmonieren und dem Zimmer einen herrschaftlichen Hauch verleihen.

Le studio est un lieu qui respire l'histoire. La table, la bibliothèque et les coffres sont des pièces anciennes très bien conservées. Les globes terrestres et les livres anciens sur la bibliothèque accentuent cette atmosphère seigneuriale.

El estudio es un lugar en el que se respira historia. La mesa, la librería y las maletas son piezas antiguas muy bien conservadas; los globos terráqueos y libros antiguos sobre la librería acentúan esta atmósfera señorial.

Lo studio è un luogo in cui si respira storia. Il tavolo, la libreria e le valigie sono pezzi antichi in ottimo stato di conservazione; i mappamondi ed i libri antichi sulla libreria accentuano questa atmosfera feudale.

Oriental Details in Brighton

☐ Bold color combinations and a colonial look are the main features of this magnificent house in the south of England. The structure of the building is in stark contrast with the decoration of its rooms. Oriental style furniture was combined with the moldings of its high ceilings and elegant curtains. Some classical armchairs and sofas were placed in one of the living rooms while another was decorated in oriental style featuring two magnificent red lacquered wardrobes. The walls in the dining room were painted in a bold violet that provides an original touch. Ballroom reminiscences are achieved in another room by using the original wooden floors, elegant curtains and the single sofa placed in this chamber.

☐ Eine gewagte Farbgebung und ein kolonialer Hauch zeichnen dieses prachtvolle Haus im Süden Englands aus. Die Architektur des Gebäudes kontrastiert mit der Dekoration der Innenräume. Asiatische Möbel werden mit den hohen Stuckdecken und eleganten Vorhängen kombiniert. In einem der Salons stehen klassische Sofas und Sessel, im anderen zwei prächtige rote Lackschränke fernöstlichen Stils. Die Wände des Esszimmers wurden in einem kühnen violetten Ton gestrichen, der die Originalität betont. Ein anderer Raum erinnert mit seinem Holzfußboden, den eleganten Gardinen und dem allein stehenden Sofa an einen Ballsaal.

☐ Couleurs osées et allure coloniale sont deux caractéristiques de cette somptueuse demeure du sud de l'Angleterre. L'architecture de l'édifice contraste avec la décoration des pièces. Des meubles de style oriental se marient aux moulures des plafonds hauts agrémentés de rideaux élégants. Un des salons décline fauteuils et divans classiques; l'autre, de style oriental, affiche deux magnifiques armoires en laqué rouge. Les murs de la salle à manger, peints d'une couleur violette audacieuse, apportent une touche d'originalité. Une autre salle rappelle un salon de danse, avec le sol en bois d'origine, d'élégants rideaux et un divan solitaire.

☐ Colores atrevidos y un aire colonial son dos rasgos de esta suntuosa vivienda del sur de Inglaterra. La arquitectura del edificio contrasta con la decoración de las estancias, en la que muebles de estilo oriental se combinan con molduras de techos altos y con elegantes cortinas. Uno de los salones tiene butacas y sofás clásicos y otro, de estilo oriental, dos magníficos armarios lacados en rojo. Las paredes del comedor se han pintado de un audaz color violeta que aporta un toque original. Otra de las salas recuerda a un salón de baile, con el suelo de madera original, elegantes cortinas y un solitario sofá.

☐ Colori audaci ed un'aria coloniale sono due degli elementi di questa sontuosa casa del sud dell'Inghilterra. L'architettura dell'edificio contrasta con l'arredamento degli ambienti. Mobili in stile orientale si abbinano con le modanature dei tetti alti e con eleganti tende. In uno dei saloni vi sono poltrone e divani classici, nell'altro, di stile orientale, due magnifici armadi laccati in rosso. Le pareti della sala da pranzo sono state dipinte in un viola molto audace che gli da un tocco originale. Un'altra delle sale ricorda un salone da ballo, con pavimento di legno originale, eleganti tendaggi ed un solitario divano.

Location: **Brighton, United Kingdom**
Decorator: **Charles Style**
Photograph © **Andreas von Einsiedel**

Feature space: **Bedroom**

The bedroom also presents an oriental style featuring an elegant screen and a piece of furniture made of dark wood at the foot of the bed. The contrast between the furniture and the classical lines of the room contributes to create a highly attractive and stylish room.

Dieses Schlafzimmer ist auch im fernöstlichen Stil eingerichtet. Hervorzuheben sind der elegante Wandschirm und das Möbelstück aus dunklem Holz am Fußende des Bettes. Durch den Kontrast der Möbel mit der klassischen Architektur entsteht ein attraktiver, eleganter Raum.

Cette chambre à coucher affiche aussi un style oriental. On y remarque un élégant paravent et un meuble en bois foncé aux pieds du lit. Le contraste produit par le mobilier et l'architecture classique de la pièce engendre une pièce séduisante et extrêmement élégante.

Este dormitorio presenta también un estilo oriental. Destacan un elegante biombo y un mueble de madera oscura a los pies de la cama. El resultado del contraste que produce el mobiliario con la arquitectura clásica de la estancia es una habitación atractiva y sumamente elegante.

Questa stanza da letto ha uno stile orientale. Spiccano un elegante séparé ed un mobile di legno scuro ai piedi del letto. Il risultato del contrasto dei mobili con l'architettura classica della stanza è un ambiente piacevole di grand'eleganza.

The combination of colors in the main bedroom features bright yellow walls against which lies a dark headboard. A daring fuchsia chaise longue was placed at the foot of the bed. Despite the apparent clash, this combination helps create a distinguished and personal room.

Das Schlafzimmer zeichnet sich durch die Kombination verschiedener Farben aus: Vor der leuchtend gelben Wand hebt sich das dunkle Kopfende ebenso ab wie die fuchsienfarbene Chaiselongue am Fuße des Bettes. Dies mag schrill erscheinen, gibt aber einen entschieden eleganten und persönlichen Touch.

Dans la chambre à coucher des maîtres, le regard est attiré par le mélange de couleurs : sur le mur peint en jaune vif, la tête de lit est foncée, aux pieds du lit, s'adosse une chaise longue dans un rose fuchsia audacieux. A priori, le résultat pourrait être criard, mais le mélange crée une pièce distinguée et personnelle.

En el dormitorio principal destaca la mezcla de colores; sobre la pared pintada de amarillo brillante hay un cabecero oscuro y a los pies de la cama, un atrevido chaise longe fucsia. A priori puede resultar estridente, pero la combinación crea una estancia distinguida y personal.

Nella stanza da letto principale spicca l'abbinamento dei colori; sulla parte dipinta in giallo brillante vi è una testata scura ed ai piedi del letto, un'originale chaise longue fucsia. A priori può sembrare stridente, ma l'abbinamento crea un ambiente elegante e personale.

Exquisite Forms

☐ This luxury home is located in one of the most exclusive quarters of London. Small details provide harmony between the different spaces. The warmth, the classical touches and the quality of its materials are key elements, and luxury can be experienced in the moldings on the ceiling, the parquet and the hall marquetry. The lavish decoration and the stylish upholstery of the living rooms bestow the large rooms with great warmth. The bathroom is light and covered with white marble tiles. Dark woods were used in one of the living rooms near the study to give the place a feeling of opulence and stateliness.

☐ Dieses luxuriöse Haus liegt in einem der vornehmsten Viertel Londons. Kleine Details tragen zu einem einheitlichen Gesamteindruck der verschiedenen Räume bei. Entscheidend sind hier die warme Stimmung, die hochwertigen Materialien, die klassischen Details und die Eleganz der Stuckdecken, des Parketts und der Intarsien des Vestibüls. Kostbare Einrichtungsgegenstände und ausgesuchte Bezugsstoffe vermögen es, selbst in einem sehr großen Raum wie dem Wohnzimmer eine äußerst gemütliche Atmosphäre zu schaffen. In einem der Salons neben dem Arbeitszimmer wurden dunkle Hölzer verwendet, um einen Eindruck herrschaftlicher Üppigkeit hervorzurufen. Das helle Bad ist in weißem Marmor gestaltet.

☐ Cette demeure luxueuse est située dans un des quartiers les plus exclusifs de Londres. Les petits détails créent l'harmonie entre les différents espaces. Chaleur, touches classiques et qualité des matériaux sont des éléments clés. Le luxe resplendit dans les moulures du plafond, le parquet et les marqueteries du vestibule. La décoration est somptueuse et les élégantes tapisseries du salon montrent qu'un très grand espace peut devenir extrêmement accueillant. La salle de bains, très lumineuse, est habillée de marbre blanc. Dans une des salles, attenante au studio, des bois aux couleurs foncées lui confèrent allure seigneuriale et opulence.

☐ Esta lujosa vivienda está situada en uno de los barrios más exclusivos de Londres. Los pequeños detalles permiten la cohesión entre los diferentes espacios; la calidez, las pinceladas clásicas y la calidad de los materiales son elementos clave y el lujo está presente en las molduras del techo, el parqué y la marquetería del vestíbulo. La decoración es suntuosa y las elegantes tapicerías del salón hacen que un espacio muy amplio pueda llegar a ser extremadamente acogedor. El baño es luminoso y está recubierto con mármol blanco. En una de las salas, junto al estudio, se han empleado maderas de tonos oscuros para darle un aire señorial y opulento.

☐ Questa casa di lusso si trova in uno dei quartieri più esclusivi di Londra. I piccoli dettagli consentono la coesione tra i vari spazi; il calore, le pennellate classiche e la qualità dei materiali sono gli elementi chiave ed il lusso invade le modanature del tetto, il parquet e la boiserie dell'ingresso. L'arredamento è sontuoso e l'elegante tappezzeria del salone fa sì che uno spazio così grande possa diventare estremamente accogliente. Il bagno, ricoperto di marmo bianco, è molto luminoso. In una delle sale, vicino allo studio, è stato usato del legno dalle tonalità scure che da alla sala un'aria maestosa ed opulenta.

Location: **London, United Kingdom**
Architect: **Weldon Washle**
Photograph © **Jonathan Moore**

Feature space: **Stairway**

The wide stairway is filled with the daylight that flows in through the windows and conveys calm and serenity. Simplicity and a classical design define the whole building. Decorative items and furniture, used sparingly, confer a stately appearance to the house.

Das geräumige Treppenhaus erhält durch die Fenster reichlich Tageslicht und strahlt Ruhe und Gelassenheit aus. Klassische Einfachheit bestimmt die Einrichtung im gesamten Haus. Die sparsam eingesetzten Möbel und anderen dekorativen Gegenstände unterstreichen die Vornehmheit des Hauses.

L'escalier est un espace large doté d'une abondance de lumière naturelle qui traverse les fenêtres, conférant calme et sérénité. Esthétique classique et dépouillement définissent l'espace entier. Le mobilier et les éléments décoratifs sont rares, mais impriment tout de même à la demeure une allure seigneuriale.

La escalera es un lugar amplio con abundante luz natural, que penetra a través de las ventanas y transmite calma y serenidad. La estética clásica y la sencillez definen el recorrido por todo el edificio. El mobiliario y los elementos decorativos son escasos, pero aun así otorgan un aspecto señorial a la vivienda.

La scala è un vano grande con abbondante luce naturale, che penetra dalle finestre e trasmette calma e serenità. L'estetica classica e la semplicità sono presenti in tutto l'edificio. I mobili e gli elementi decorativi sono limitati, ma pur così conferiscono un aspetto maestoso alla casa.

The kitchen is located next to the dining room. The large swing doors separate the two spaces but keep the moldings and the parquet floor as common elements, thus creating a stately and classical atmosphere.

Die Küche liegt neben dem Esszimmer und ist von diesem durch eine große Flügeltür getrennt. Beide Räume weisen Stuckverzierungen an der Decke und Parkettboden auf und erhalten dadurch eine herrschaftliche Atmosphäre.

La cuisine est à côté de la salle à manger. Une grande porte à deux battants sépare ces deux espaces qui partagent certains éléments communs, à l'instar des moulures aux plafonds et du parquet, reproduisant ainsi la même atmosphère seigneuriale et classique.

La cocina se encuentra junto al comedor. Una gran puerta de dos alas separa estos dos espacios, que mantienen como elementos comunes las molduras en los techos y el suelo de parqué, y crean, de este modo, una misma atmósfera señorial y clásica.

La cucina si trova vicino alla sala da pranzo. Una gran porta a due battenti separa questi due spazi, che hanno come elementi comuni le modanature dei tetti ed il pavimento in parquet, e creano, in tal modo, una stessa atmosfera maestosa e classica.

An Apartment in San Sebastián

☐ This elegant and luminous home was recently refurbished and transformed into a luxury apartment in order to meet the needs of the couple who owns it. Partitions were removed to change the layout of the rooms, which allowed for a living room, a main double bedroom with a dressing room and two contiguous bathrooms (one for each partner), a guest room, a study and a kitchen area. White is the predominant color of this home, which enhances luminosity and gives a feeling of amplitude, in contrast with the light gray used in the floors of some rooms and the main bathroom. Lighting has been successfully used by using halogen lamps on the ceilings and at floor level, thus creating a sophisticated interplay of lights and shadows.

☐ Diese helle, elegante Wohnung ist kürzlich in ein luxuriöses Apartment umgestaltet worden, um den Ansprüchen des Besitzerpaars zu genügen. Viele Trennwände wurden herausgerissen, die Raumverteilung neu organisiert. Es wurden ein Wohnzimmer und ein Schlafzimmer mit Ankleidezimmer und zwei nebeneinander liegenden Badezimmern eingerichtet. Außerdem gibt es ein Gästezimmer, ein Arbeitszimmer und die Office-Küche. Das überall vorherrschende Weiß schafft Helle und Weite und steht in Kontrast zu den grauen Böden einiger Zimmer und des Bades. Auf die Ausleuchtung wurde besonderer Wert gelegt: Die Halogenleuchten an der Decke und kurz über dem Boden erzeugen ein reizvolles Licht- und Schattenspiel.

☐ Cette demeure élégante et lumineuse a été récemment restaurée pour satisfaire aux besoins de ses propriétaires, un couple, et se convertir en un appartement luxueux. Les cloisons ont été éliminées et les pièces réorganisées. Un salon, une chambre à coucher de maître avec un dressing et deux salles de bains doubles (une pour chacun), une chambre à coucher d'amis, un bureau et une cuisine-office, ont été réhabilités. Le blanc qui domine dans toute la maison, apporte clarté et largesse et contraste avec la douceur du gris du sol dans certaines pièces et dans la salle de bains principale. L'éclairage est aussi une réussite : lampes halogènes au plafond et à ras du sol créent un jeu sophistiqué d'ombres et de lumières.

☐ Esta elegante y luminosa vivienda se ha reformado recientemente para satisfacer las necesidades de sus propietarios, una pareja, y se ha convertido en un lujoso piso. Se han eliminado tabiques y se han redistribuido las estancias; se ha habilitado un salón, un dormitorio principal con vestidor y dos baños unidos (uno para cada uno), un dormitorio de invitados, un despacho y una cocina-office. El blanco predomina en toda la casa, aporta claridad y amplitud, y contrasta con el suave gris del suelo en algunas estancias y en el baño principal. La iluminación es otro de los aciertos: luces halógenas en techos y a ras de suelo crean un sofisticado juego de luces y sombras.

☐ Quest'elegante appartamento molto luminoso è stato recentemente ristrutturato per soddisfare le necessità della coppia di proprietari, ed è diventato un appartamento di lusso. Sono stati eliminati i tramezzi e ridistribuiti gli ambienti; si è ricavato un salone, una stanza da letto principale con spogliatoio e due bagni uniti (uno per ognuno), una stanza per invitati, un ufficio ed una cucina-office. In tutta la casa predomina il bianco, che da luminosità e sensazione di spazio, e che contrasta con il grigio tenue del pavimento di alcune stanze e del bagno principale. L'illuminazione è un'altra delle scelte felici: luci alogene sui tetti ed a livello del pavimento per creare un sofisticato gioco di luci ed ombre.

Location: San Sebastián, Spain
Decorator: Ania Azcárate
Photograph © Montse Garriga

Feature space: Distributor

A small distributor provides amplitude thanks to the flow of light and the mirrors that create an illusion of expansion in the room, as if going through glass doors. This space is an example of the classical style and simplicity of this home.

Das einfallende Licht und die Spiegel, die es geschickt vervielfältigen, als käme es durch Glastüren, vermitteln dem kleinen Flur eine gewisse Weitläufigkeit. Die hier erkennbare klassische Schlichtheit herrscht in der gesamten Wohnung vor.

Une petite entrée élargit l'espace grâce à l'afflux de lumière et aux miroirs qui l'agrandissent, donne l'impression de traverser des portes en verre. Cet espace est un échantillon du style classique et de la simplicité qui se dégage de la demeure.

Un pequeño distribuidor aporta amplitud gracias a la entrada de luz y a unos espejos que la expanden como si atravesara unas puertas acristaladas. Este espacio es una muestra del estilo clásico y de la sencillez que se respira en la vivienda.

Un piccolo disimpegno da una sensazione di spazio grazie alla luce che entra, ed agli specchi che ne amplificano l'effetto, come se si attraversassero porte vetrate. Questo spazio è un esempio di stile classico e della semplicità che si respira in tutto l'appartamento.

The furniture consists of antiques that belong to the owners and other furniture designed by the decorator. In the bathroom, a bust made of stone contributes to the classical ambiance and puts the emphasis on traditional decoration.

Das Apartment ist mit antiken Möbeln aus Familienbesitz und anderen, von der Innenarchitektin entworfenen Stücken ausgestattet. Die steinerne Büste im Bad trägt mit zu der klassisch-traditionellen Atmosphäre der Wohnung bei.

Le mobilier se compose de pièces anciennes appartenant au propriétaire et d'autres meubles conçus par la décoratrice. Dans la salle de bains, un buste de pierre contribue à créer une ambiance classique et exalte la décoration traditionnelle.

El mobiliario está compuesto por piezas antiguas que pertenecen a los propietarios y por otros muebles diseñados por la decoradora. En el baño un busto de piedra contribuye a crear un ambiente clásico y subraya la decoración tradicional.

L'arredamento è composto di pezzi antichi dei proprietari e da altri mobili disegnati dall'arredatrice. In bagno un busto in pietra ricrea un ambiente classico, mettendo in evidenza l'arredamento tradizionale.

An Apartment in London

☐ This luxurious apartment has a sophisticated atmosphere. A feeling of serenity is conveyed by using classical elements, such as the Ionic columns of the hall, as well as by the orderly layout of the space and the furniture arrangement. Rich carpets are placed to demarcate the different areas of the living room. The main bathroom is decorated in brown marble, and is an example of the choice of classicism made for the whole house. The oak wood paneled distributor transforms an area of transit into a library. The interior features predominantly a choice of objects of good taste.

☐ Hinter der Ausstattung dieses klar gegliederten Apartments stehen die Ideen eines anspruchsvollen Eigentümers. Die Einrichtung greift auf klassische Elemente wie die ionischen Säulen im Vestibül zurück und die Möbel strahlen eine gewisse Gelassenheit aus. Prachtvolle Teppiche begrenzen die einzelnen Bereiche im Wohnzimmer. Das mit braunem Marmor ausgekleidete Badezimmer ist ein gutes Beispiel für den Klassizismus der Wohnung. Die Diele wird durch das eingebaute Eichenregal von einem Durchgangszimmer zu einer eleganten Bibliothek. Überall in diesem geschmackvoll eingerichteten Haus entdeckt man interessante Details.

☐ Une atmosphère précieuse définit cet appartement luxueux. La décoration est basée sur des éléments classiques, à l'instar des colonnes ioniques du vestibule, et la distribution régulière de l'espace et du mobilier confère une certaine sérénité. De magnifiques tapis délimitent les différentes zones du salon. La salle de bains principale, décorée de marbre marron, est un exemple supplémentaire du classicisme qui émane de toute la maison. Dans le hall d'entrée, les boiseries en chêne métamorphosent la pièce en une élégante bibliothèque, sublimant cette zone de passage. L'intérieur déborde de détails de bon goût.

☐ Una atmósfera sofisticada define este lujoso apartamento. La decoración se basa en elementos clásicos, como las columnas jónicas del vestíbulo, y la ordenada distribución del espacio y del mobiliario transmite cierta serenidad. Se han colocado unas magníficas alfombras para delimitar las diferentes áreas del salón. El baño principal, decorado con mármol marrón, es un ejemplo más del clasicismo que se respira en toda la casa. En el distribuidor, una boiserie de roble convierte la estancia en una elegante biblioteca, además de una zona de paso. Así pues, el interior está repleto de detalles en los que predomina el buen gusto.

☐ Un'atmosfera sofisticata definisce questo appartamento di lusso. L'arredamento si basa su elementi classici, come le colonne ioniche dell'atrio, e la curata distribuzione dello spazio e dei mobili che trasmette una certa serenità. Le varie zone del salone sono state delimitate da magnifici tappeti. Il bagno principale, decorato con marmo marrone, è un esempio in più del classicismo che si respira in tutta la casa. Nel disimpegno, una "boiserie" di rovere trasforma l'ambiente in un'elegante biblioteca, oltre a zona di passaggio. Così dunque, l'interno è pieno di dettagli tra i quali predomina il buon gusto.

Location: **London, United Kingdom**
Decorator: **Thornsett Group**
Photograph © **Carlos Dominguez**

Feature space: **Main bedroom**

The main bedroom is a grand chamber in which a bed with a canopy has been placed as a main feature. The fireplace, the swinging mirror and the chests of drawers are reminiscent of a stately past while each lavish detail transforms the room into a cozy and friendly place.

Das Schlafzimmer ist ein sehenswerter Raum mit einem Himmelbett als bestimmendem Einrichtungsstück. Der Kamin, der schwenkbare Spiegel und die Kommoden beschwören eine herrschaftliche Vergangenheit herauf, und ausgesuchte Details schaffen Gemütlichkeit.

La chambre à coucher des maîtres est un espace magnifique dotée d'un lit à baldaquin, qui en est la pièce maîtresse. La cheminée, le miroir basculant et les commodes évoquent un passé seigneurial et les détails luxueux métamorphosent la pièce en un lieu agréable et accueillant.

El dormitorio principal es una ostentosa estancia con una cama con baldaquín como pieza principal. La chimenea, el espejo basculante y las cómodas evocan un pasado señorial, y los lujosos detalles convierten la estancia en un lugar agradable y acogedor.

La stanza da letto principale è un ambiente splendido con un letto a baldacchino come elemento principale. Il camino, lo specchio oscillante ed i cassettoni evocano un passato maestoso, mentre i lussuosi dettagli trasformano la stanza in un luogo gradevole ed accogliente.

The stylish decoration of the dining room is a clear example of the classical style: the moldings of the ceiling, the crystal chandelier and the candelabra are only a few examples.

Zur eleganten Einrichtung des Esszimmers im klassischen Stil gehören die Stuckdecken, der Kristallleuchter und die Kandelaber.

L'élégante décoration de la salle à manger est d'un pur style classique : les moulures du plafond, le lustre aux gouttes de cristal et les chandeliers n'en sont que quelques exemples.

La elegante decoración del comedor es de un claro estilo clásico; las molduras del techo, la lámpara de lágrimas de cristal y los candelabros son tan sólo algunos ejemplos.

L'elegante arredamento della sala da pranzo è in chiaro stile classico; le modanature del tetto, la lampada di lacrime di cristallo ed i candelabri ne sono solo alcuni esempi.

London Tradition

☐ This smart apartment is full of details such as the classical and distinguished moldings of its ceiling. Soft colors in neuter tones help create light rooms with an overall feel of serenity. A few selected pieces of old furniture provide a delicate and airy atmosphere. The bedrooms are filled with comfort and warmth, featuring fireplaces and flower-patterned wallpapers. The precious daylight, which is scarce in this city, is captured by a skylight in a small dining room. A leafy terrace provides an attractive space for outdoor enjoyment.

☐ Stuckdecken und andere Details in diesem eleganten Apartment sind typisch für den distinguierten klassischen Stil. Zurückhaltende, neutrale Farbtöne schaffen helle, heitere Räume. An einigen Stellen findet man geschickt platzierte antike Möbelstücke, die eine eigene Wirkung entfalten. Die gemütlichen Schlafräume sind mit Kaminen und mit geblümten Tapeten ausgestattet. Das kleine Esszimmer wird durch ein Oberlicht zu einem, lichtdurchfluteten Raum – eine Kostbarkeit in dieser Stadt – und eine Terrasse mit vielen Pflanzen bietet einen attraktiven Platz, um Momente unter freiem Himmel zu genießen.

☐ Cet élégant appartement déborde de détails, à l'instar des moulures du plafond, emprunts d'un style distingué et classique. Les couleurs douces, aux tonalités neutres, créent des pièces lumineuses et dégagent une sensation de sérénité. Les meubles anciens sont présents, même s'ils ne sont pas excessifs et font que l'atmosphère est délicate et sobre. Les chambres à coucher, pièces pratiques et accueillantes, ont une cheminée et des murs décorés de papier peint aux motifs floraux. Une petite salle à manger dotée d'un velux bénéficie au maximum de la lumière naturelle, très précieuse dans cette ville, et une terrasse débordante de plantes offre un espace charmant pour profiter de l'extérieur.

☐ Este elegante apartamento está repleto de detalles, como las molduras del techo, que muestran un estilo distinguido y clásico. Los colores suaves, de tonos neutros, crean estancias luminosas y producen sensación de serenidad. Los muebles antiguos están presentes, aunque no en exceso, y hacen que la atmósfera sea delicada y sencilla. Los dormitorios, estancias cómodas y acogedoras, tienen chimenea y papel pintado con motivos florales en las paredes. Un pequeño comedor con una claraboya aprovecha al máximo la luz natural, muy preciada en esta ciudad, y una terraza repleta de plantas proporciona un atractivo espacio para disfrutar del exterior.

☐ Questo elegante appartamento è pieno di dettagli, come le modanature del tetto, che mostrano uno stile elegante e classico. I colori morbidi, dai toni neutri, creano ambienti luminosi e producono una sensazione di serenità. I mobili antichi sono presenti, ma senza esagerare, e rendono l'atmosfera delicata e semplice. Le stanze da letto, ambienti comodi ed accoglienti, contano con camino e pareti rivestite con carta parati dai motivi floreali. Una piccola sala da pranzo con un lucernaio sfrutta al massimo la luce naturale, molto apprezzata in questa città, ed un terrazzo pieno di piante offre un bello spazio per godersi l'aria pura.

Location: **London, United Kingdom**
Decorator: **Grady Cooley**
Photograph © **Andreas von Einsiedel**

Feature space: **Living room**

The living room is one of the smartest rooms of this house, featuring the moldings in the ceiling and a grand fireplace presided by a mirror with a carved frame, all of which contributes to create a sumptuous yet balanced place.

Der Salon ist einer der elegantesten Räume des Hauses, wie sich an den Stuckverzierungen der Decke, dem vornehmen Kamin und dem darüber aufgehängten, verzierten Spiegel zeigt: ein reichhaltig, aber ausgewogen ausgestattetes Zimmer.

Le salon est une des plus élégantes pièces de la maison, doté de remarquables moulures au plafond et d'une cheminée distinguée sur laquelle repose un miroir au cadre ouvragé : un espace somptueux mais tout en harmonie.

El salón es una de las estancias más elegantes de la casa, donde destacan las molduras del techo y la distinguida chimenea sobre la que se ha colocado un espejo con un gran marco labrado: un espacio suntuoso pero equilibrado.

Il salone è uno degli ambienti più eleganti della casa, in cui spiccano le modanature del tetto, e l'elegante camino sul quale svetta uno specchio con una gran cornice lavorata: uno spazio sontuoso ma equilibrato.

Bedrooms are profusely decorated with painted wallpapers bearing the same pattern as the one used in the curtains. Stately chests of drawers and other items of furniture complete the rooms, one of which features a stylish fireplace.

Die Schlafräume sind reich dekoriert; die Tapeten haben das gleiche Muster wie die Vorhänge. Wertvolle Kommoden und andere Möbelstücke ergänzen die Einrichtung der Zimmer, von denen eines sogar einen prachtvollen Kamin hat.

Les chambres à coucher sont abondamment décorées, avec des papiers peints aux murs dont le motif est assorti aux rideaux. Commodes luxueuses et autres pièces de mobilier complètent les pièces, l'une d'entre elles étant parée d'une somptueuse cheminée.

Los dormitorios están profusamente decorados, con papeles pintados sobre las paredes que tienen el mismo estampado que las cortinas. Lujosas cómodas y otras piezas de mobiliario completan las estancias, y una de ellas dispone incluso de una lujosa chimenea.

Le stanze da letto profusamente arredate, presentano sulle pareti della carta parati con lo stesso stampato delle tende. Lussuosi cassettoni ed altri pezzi completano gli ambienti. In uno spicca uno splendido camino.

Extreme Classicism

☐ Opulence and classicism are the marks of this residence. The hall features two impressive semicircular arches that confer a palatial aspect to it and the rest of the transit areas are decorated with exquisite taste, too. The furniture and the curtains contribute to create an atmosphere of lavishness and warmth in all the rooms, which are also enhanced with the rich moldings in the ceilings and fireplaces. The bathrooms of classical design are covered in marble and present a contrast with the kitchen, the only room that steps away from classical style, yet always maintaining the same overall stylishness of the rest of house.

☐ Üppigkeit und Klassizismus zeichnen diese Wohnung aus. Das Vestibül ist mit zwei eindrucksvollen Rundbögen geschmückt, die an einen Palast erinnern. Selbst alle Durchgangsräume sind sehr geschmackvoll eingerichtet. Möbel und Vorhänge strahlen eine luxuriöse Behaglichkeit aus, die durch den reichverzierten Stuck an Decken und Kaminen noch verstärkt wird. Die klassisch gestalteten Badezimmer sind mit Marmor ausgekleidet, während sich die Küche als einziger Raum der Wohnung von der klassizistischen Linie entfernt, ohne jedoch auf Eleganz zu verzichten.

☐ Opulence et classicisme sont les deux traits qui définissent cette résidence. Le vestibule dispose de deux impressionnants arcs en plein cintre aux allures de palais et les autres zones de passage sont décorées avec un goût exquis. Le mobilier et les rideaux impriment les pièces de chaleur et de splendeur, exaltées par les merveilleuses moulures apparentes sur les plafonds comme sur les cheminées. Les salles de bains, aux lignes classiques, sont revêtues de marbre et contrastent avec la cuisine, l'unique pièce qui se démarque de ce classicisme, tout en maintenant l'élégance du reste de la maison.

☐ Opulencia y clasicismo son dos de los rasgos que definen esta residencia. El vestíbulo tiene dos imponentes arcos de medio punto de aspecto palaciego y el resto de las zonas de paso están decoradas asimismo con un gusto exquisito. El mobiliario y los cortinajes aportan suntuosidad y calidez a las estancias, acentuadas por las ricas molduras que se pueden ver tanto en techos como en chimeneas. Los baños, de líneas clásicas, están revestidos con mármoles y contrastan con la cocina, la única estancia que se desmarca de este clasicismo, pero manteniendo la elegancia del resto de la casa.

☐ Opulenza e classicismo sono due degli elementi che definiscono questa residenza. L'atrio presenta due imponenti archi a tutto sesto d'aspetto imponente ed anche il resto delle zone di passaggio sono decorate con squisito gusto. I mobili e le tende conferiscono sontuosità e calore agli ambienti, il tutto accentuato da ricche modanature sui tetti e sui camini. I bagni, dalle linee classiche sono rivestiti con marmi e contrastano con la cucina, l'unico ambiente che si stacca dal classico, mantenendo però l'eleganza del resto della casa.

Location: **London, United Kingdom**
Architect: **Weldon Washle**
Photograph © **Jonathan Moore**

Feature space: **Transit areas**

The parquet and the walls of the transit areas are also covered in wood, thus emphasizing the feeling of warmth and comfort. The stone busts in the distributor confer a refined and stately aspect to the room that leads to the study.

Die Parkettfußböden und die holzgetäfelten Wände des Übergangsbereichs vermitteln angenehme Behaglichkeit. Steinerne Büsten im Flur geben diesem Bereich, der in das Arbeitszimmer führt, eine raffiniert vornehme Note.

Le parquet et les murs des zones de passage sont également habillés de bois, soulignant ainsi la sensation de chaleur et de commodité. Les bustes de pierre du hall de réception impriment un caractère seigneurial et raffiné à une pièce qui mène au studio.

El suelo de parqué y las paredes de las zonas de paso también están revestidas con madera, y subrayan así la sensación de calidez y comodidad. Unos bustos de piedra en el distribuidor otorgan un aspecto señorial y refinado a una estancia que conduce al estudio.

Il pavimento di parquet e le pareti delle zone di passaggio sono anch'esse rivestite di legno, e sottolineano così la sensazione di calore e confort. Dei busti in pietra nel disimpegno conferiscono un aspetto maestoso e raffinato ad un ambiente che porta allo studio.

This living room has a lavish French style decoration. The sophisticated armchairs and side tables, the curtains, and even the canvas hanging over the fireplace are of French inspiration, which creates a period atmosphere.

Dieser Wohnraum sticht durch seine äußerst prachtvolle französische Dekoration hervor. Die edlen Sessel und distinguierten Beistelltischchen, die Vorhänge und sogar das Gemälde über dem Kamin sind französisch inspiriert und so fühlt man sich in eine andere Zeit versetzt.

Ce salon attire l'attention pour sa décoration extrêmement somptueuse, de style français. Les fauteuils très travaillés et les tables d'appoint, les rideaux, y compris la toile au-dessus de la cheminée, tous d'inspiration française, nous transposent dans une autre époque.

Este salón destaca por una decoración extremadamente suntuosa y de estilo francés. Las sofisticadas butacas y mesas auxiliares, los cortinajes, e incluso el lienzo sobre la chimenea, son de inspiración francesa y dan la sensación de estar en otra época.

Questo salone spicca per un arredamento estremamente sontuoso e di stile francese. Le sofisticate poltrone ed i tavolini ausiliari, le tende, ed anche la tela sul camino sono d'ispirazione francese e danno la sensazione di trovarsi in un'altra epoca.

Lambert Residence

☐ This magnificent residence was designed in Georgian style, one of the most preferred and prominent styles in Palm Beach for its elegance. A billiard room and projection hall were created, adding character to the residence and giving it a modern touch despite its overall traditional style. Large windows ensure the flow of daylight and combine neutral colors with tropical style furniture. French doors open to the outside where a magnificent swimming-pool lies in the middle of a finely-kept garden. The magnificent wine cellar area was specially designed to resemble the atmosphere of a French chateau.

☐ Dieses prächtige Anwesen wurde im georgianischen Stil errichtet, der aufgrund seiner Eleganz ein in Palm Beach bevorzugter Stil ist. Obwohl im ganzen Haus ein traditioneller Stil vorherrscht, zeigt die Einrichtung eines Billardsaals und eines Vorführraums, dass man das Haus den persönlichen Bedürfnissen anzupassen weiß. Die Innenräume erhalten durch die großen Fenster viel Tageslicht, das die tropischen Möbel vor der neutral gehaltenen Einrichtung gut zur Wirkung kommen lässt. Türen im französischen Stil öffnen das Haus nach draußen zu den gepflegten Gärten mit dem großzügigen Schwimmbecken. Der eindrucksvolle Weinkeller wurde im Stile der französischen Châteaus gestaltet.

☐ Cette splendide résidence, conçue dans le style géorgien, est une des plus remarquables de Palm Beach pour son élégance. Une salle de billard et une autre de projection ont été reconverties, donnant un certain cachet et une allure moderne à cette demeure, en dépit du style traditionnel qui prime dans toute la maison. L'intérieur est inondé de lumière naturelle grâces aux baies vitrées et combine les couleurs neutres à un mobilier tropical. Des portes de style français permettent d'ouvrir la maison sur l'extérieur, doté de jardins très bien entretenus et d'une somptueuse piscine. La cave est un magnifique espace, travaillé d'une certaine manière pour reproduire l'atmosphère d'un « château » à la Française.

☐ Esta espléndida residencia ha sido diseñada siguiendo el estilo georgiano, uno de los más prominentes en Palm Beach por su elegancia. Se ha habilitado una sala de billar y otra de proyección, que personalizan la vivienda y le dan un aire moderno, a pesar del estilo tradicional que impera en toda la casa. El interior dispone de abundante luz natural gracias a los ventanales y combina los colores neutros con mobiliario tropical. Unas puertas de estilo francés permiten abrir la casa al exterior, donde se encuentran unos cuidados jardines y una suntuosa piscina. La bodega es un magnífico espacio sobre el que se trabajó de manera especial para reproducir la atmósfera de un "chateau" francés.

☐ Questa splendida residenza è stata disegnata seguendo lo stile georgiano, uno dei più presenti a Palm Beach per la sua eleganza. E' stata creata una sala da biliardo ed un'altra di proiezione, che personalizzano la casa conferendogli un'aria moderna, nonostante lo stile tradizionale che impera ovunque. Gli interni godono di un'abbondante luce naturale grazie ai finestroni ed abbina i colori neutri con mobili tropicali. Delle porte di stile francese consentono di aprire la casa verso l'esterno, dove si trovano dei giardini ben curati ed una sontuosa piscina. La cantina è uno spazio magnifico curato in modo speciale per riprodurre l'atmosfera di un "château" francese.

Location: **Palm Beach, United States**
Architect: **Thomas M. Kirchhoff**
Decorator: **Amy H. Pagano**
Photograph © **Sargent Architectural Photography**

Feature space: **Cellar**

As the house lies on an elevated site, a magnificent cellar was made in the basement that can store up to 2.500 bottles. Carved oak wood beams and vaulted ceilings contribute to a feeling of amplitude, in spite of the lack of windows, while a table made of African railway ties provides an original touch.

Die Lage des Hauses auf einer Anhöhe erlaubte die Einrichtung eines Weinkellers im Untergeschoss, der bis zu 2500 Flaschen aufnehmen kann. Eichenbalken und die gewölbte Decke lassen trotz der fehlenden Fenster kein Gefühl der Enge aufkommen, und der Tisch aus afrikanischen Eisenbahnschwellen stellt ein originelles Detail dar.

La situation en hauteur du lieu a permis d'installer une magnifique cave au sous-sol, d'une contenance de 2.500 bouteilles. Poutres de chêne travaillées et plafond voûté confèrent une sensation de largesse malgré l'absence de fenêtres. Une table faite de traverses de rails de chemin de fer africains apporte à l'ensemble une touche d'originalité.

La elevación del lugar permitió habilitar una magnífica bodega en el sótano, con capacidad para 2.500 botellas. Vigas de roble labradas y techos abovedados producen sensación de amplitud, a pesar de no haber ventanas, y una mesa de traviesas de vías de tren africanas aporta un toque original al conjunto.

L'elevazione del luogo ha permesso di creare una magnifica cantina nel piano interrato, con capienza per 2500 bottiglie. Travi di legno lavorato e tetti a volta offrono una sensazione di spazio, pur in assenza di finestre, ed un tavolo di traversine di binari provenienti dall'Africa danno un tocco originale all'ambiente.

Profusely decorated with rich upholstery and curtains, the living room confers lavish distinction to the interior. The comfortable sofas and armchairs enhance the cozy ambiance and the stateliness that impregnates the house.

Der Salon ist ein üppig ausgeschmückter, behaglicher Raum mit eleganten Polster- und Vorhangsstoffen, in dem die bequemen Sitzgarnituren die im ganzen Haus zu spürende luxuriös-herrschaftliche, aber warme Atmosphäre betonen.

Le salon est une pièce abondamment décorée de merveilleux rideaux et tapisseries tout en élégance conférant distinction et somptuosité à l'intérieur. Divans et fauteuils confortables accentuent l'allure chaleureuse et seigneuriale qui émane de toute la demeure.

El salón es una estancia profusamente decorada con ricas y elegantes tapicerías y cortinas que otorgan distinción y suntuosidad al interior. Confortables sofás y butacas acentúan la calidez y el aire señorial que se respira en toda la vivienda.

Il salone è una sala profusamente decorata con tappezzerie e tendaggi ricchi ed eleganti che conferiscono distinzione e sontuosità all'ambiente. Dei comodi divani e poltrone accentuano il calore e l'aspetto maestoso che si respira in tutta la casa.

Brightness and Simplicity

☐ This warm and friendly house has a classical decoration and appears to be plain. However, the arrangement of the stylish furniture was made in accordance with light, thus providing liveliness to its rooms. Every detail of the furniture of the rooms was taken care of to achieve delicate ambiances filled with great style. The light tones employed throughout the house confer charm and distinction to it. The large living rooms are connected and provide varied luxurious spaces while respecting a unity of style. An antique table is placed in the library to create a work area.

☐ Diese einladende Wohnung zeichnet sich durch ihre klassische Dekoration aus. Die hellen, eher schlichten Räume werden durch die Anordnung der ausgesuchten Möbel mit Leben erfüllt. Bei der Auswahl des Mobiliars wurden auch noch so kleine Details beachtet, um einen stilistisch stimmigen Gesamteindruck zu erzielen. In der Farbpalette herrschen helle Töne vor, die dem ganzen Haus eine anziehende Kultiviertheit verleihen. Die weitläufigen Wohnräume gehen ineinander über und so entstehen ganz eigene, doch von einem einheitlichen Stil geprägte Bereiche. In der Bibliothek wurde ein prachtvoller alter Tisch als Arbeitsplatz aufgestellt.

☐ Cette habitation accueillante et chaleureuse se définit par une décoration classique. L'élégance dans la disposition du mobilier et la luminosité des pièces remplissent la maison de dynamisme, dans un dépouillement apparent. Toutefois, un soin particulier dans le choix du mobilier des salles permet d'obtenir des ambiances délicates et très stylées. Les tons clairs dominent la palette des couleurs de toute la maison, lui conférant distinction et charme. Les vastes salons communiquent et créent des espaces luxueux, différents, tout en conservant une unité de style. L'un d'eux accueille la bibliothèque, parée d'une splendide table ancienne, créant le coin bureau.

☐ Esta acogedora y cálida vivienda se define por una decoración clásica. La elegancia en la disposición del mobiliario y la luminosidad de las estancias llenan de vitalidad la casa, aparentemente sencilla. Sin embargo, se han cuidado todos los detalles en el mobiliario de las salas para conseguir unos ambientes delicados y con mucho estilo. Los tonos claros dominan la paleta de colores de toda la casa y le confieren distinción y atractivo. Los amplios salones se comunican y crean espacios lujosos y diferentes, aunque con un estilo unitario. Uno de ellos es la biblioteca, donde se ha colocado una espléndida mesa antigua para crear una zona de trabajo.

☐ Questa casa accogliente e calda si definisce con un arredamento classico. L'eleganza nella disposizione dei mobili e la luminosità degli ambienti colmano di vitalità la casa, apparentemente semplice. Tutti i dettagli dei mobili delle sale sono stati curati per ottenere degli ambienti delicati e con molto stile. I toni chiari predominano sui colori di tutta la casa, dandogli un aspetto distinto ed attraente. I grandi saloni sono comunicanti e creano spazi lussuosi e diversi, ma con uno stile unico. In uno si trova la biblioteca, con uno splendido tavolo antico per creare una zona di lavoro.

Location: **London, United Kingdom**

Decorator: **Lesley Cooke**

Photograph © **Andreas von Einsiedel**

Feature space: **Living room**

This residence has three rooms connected with each other. The fireplace is located in the first room, which has also a piano; the second room is the library, which has a large bookcase and a small antique desk; the third room is a living room with sofas and armchairs in different styles.

In dieser Wohnung gibt es drei miteinander verbundene Salons. Im ersten Zimmer mit Kamin steht das Klavier, der zweite dient mit einem großen Bücherschrank und einem kleinen Schreibtisch als Bibliothek, der dritte schließlich lädt mit Sofas und Sesseln in unterschiedlichen Stilen zum Plaudern ein.

Cette résidence dispose de trois salons communicants entre eux. Le premier salon, dotée d'une cheminée, accueille le piano. Le deuxième, héberge une bibliothèque et une petite écritoire ancienne. Enfin, le troisième est une salle parée de divans et de fauteuils de différents styles.

Esta residencia dispone de tres salones comunicados entre sí. En el primer salón, con chimenea, se encuentra el piano; en el segundo, que actúa como biblioteca, una gran librería y un pequeño escritorio antiguo; finalmente, el tercero es una sala con sofás y butacas de diferentes estilos.

Questa residenza dispone di una fuga di tre saloni. Nel primo, con camino, vi è il piano; nel secondo, che funge da biblioteca, una grande libreria ed un piccolo scrittoio antico; infine, il terzo, è una sala con divani e poltrone di stili vari.

The main bedroom, with a door that leads to an inconspicuous bathroom, is small but the delicate furniture and the choice of materials help create an elegant room. The shower, the washbasin, the shelves and other elements are arranged to form an alley leading to the living rooms.

Das Schlafzimmer der Eigentümer hat direkten Zugang zu einem versteckten Bad. Der Schlafraum ist zwar klein, aber die ausgesuchten Möbel und Materialien verleihen ihm eigenen Glanz. Die Dusche, das Waschbecken, die Regale und weitere Elemente wurden so angeordnet, dass sie einen Gang bilden, der in die Salons führt.

La chambre à coucher des maîtres, attenante à une salle de bains discrète, est petite, mais la finesse du mobilier et des matériaux configurent une pièce tout en élégance. La douche, le lave-mains, les étagères et autres éléments sont disposés, à l'instar d'un couloir qui mène aux salons.

El dormitorio principal, con acceso a un discreto baño, es pequeño, pero la delicadeza del mobiliario y de los materiales configuran una elegante estancia. La ducha, el lavamanos, los estantes y demás elementos se han dispuesto formando un pasillo que conduce a los salones.

La stanza da letto principale, che accede ad un discreto bagno, è piccola, ma la delicatezza dei mobili e dei materiali scelti conferiscono eleganza all'ambiente. La doccia, il lavandino, le mensole e gli altri elementi sono stati disposti in modo da formare un corridoio che porta ai saloni.

The dining room combines simple decorative objects with other items of great sophistication, such as the successful combination of a crystal chandelier with simple Japanese flowers and candelabra.

Im Esszimmer sind verschiedene schlichte dekorative Gegenstände mit prachtvolleren Elementen auf anspruchsvolle Weise miteinander kombiniert worden, wie z. B. ein Leuchter mit Kristallgehängen mit einfachen Kerzenhaltern und japanischen Blumen.

La salle à manger réunit des objets décoratifs d'une grande sobriété, à d'autres plus sophistiqués, associant à merveille un lustre en gouttes de cristal à de simples candélabres et à des fleurs japonaises.

El comedor reúne objetos decorativos de gran sencillez con otros más sofisticados, combinando con gran acierto una lámpara de lágrimas de cristal con sencillos candelabros y flores japonesas.

La sala da pranzo presenta oggetti decorativi di grande semplicità ed altri più sofisticati, abbinando con successo una lampada di lacrime di cristallo con semplici candelabri e fiori giapponesi.

Portman Residence

☐ This spectacular loft is located in Tribeca, a fashionable borough in the avant-garde of culture. East meets West in this residence that exemplifies of elegance and style, and opts for a minimalist look complemented by a collection of Asian antiques. Furniture is limited to the essential, always harmonizing with the art collection that combines Buddha statues with a painting by Chagall. As the original space was altered, great attention was given to detail; building materials and part of the furniture were imported from Florence. The terrace features a small granite pool of Asian inspiration with a magnificent view of the skyline of this quarter.

☐ Dieses spektakuläre Loft liegt in Tribeca, einem der beliebtesten Viertel der kulturellen Avantgarde. Morgenland und Abendland vereinen sich in dieser stilvollen Wohnung, die gekennzeichnet ist durch die Vorliebe für die minimalistische Ästhetik und eine Kollektion asiatischer Antiquitäten. Das spärliche Mobiliar harmoniert mit der Kunstsammlung, die Buddhastatuetten, aber auch ein Bild von Chagall umfasst. Die ursprüngliche Raumaufteilung wurde verändert und bei der Neugestaltung wurde größter Wert auf Details gelegt. Die Materialien und ein Großteil der Möbel kommen aus Florenz. Von der Terrasse mit ihrem kleinen Wasserbecken aus Granit im asiatischen Stil genießt man den Blick auf die Skyline des Viertels.

☐ Ce loft spectaculaire se trouve à Tribeca, un des quartiers les plus à la mode pour être à l'avant-garde culturelle. L'orient et l'occident s'unissent dans cette demeure avec élégance et style, au travers de l'engouement pour l'esthétique minimaliste et d'une collection d'antiquités asiatiques. Le mobilier est réduit au minimum et s'harmonise à la collection d'art, qui conjugue statues de Bouddha et un cadre de Chagall. L'espace original a été modifié, avec un soin remarquable du détail. Les matériaux de construction, ainsi qu'une grande partie du mobilier, viennent de Florence. La terrasse, dotée d'une petite piscine de granit à l'esthétique orientale, offre de fantastiques vues sur la « sky line » du quartier.

☐ Este espectacular loft se encuentra en Tribeca, uno de los barrios más de moda por estar a la vanguardia cultural. Oriente y occidente se funden en esta vivienda con elegancia y estilo, puesto que confluyen en ella el gusto por la estética minimalista y una colección de antigüedades asiáticas. El mobiliario es mínimo y armoniza con la colección de arte, que combina estatuas de Buda con un cuadro de Chagall. Se ha modificado el espacio original, cuidando al máximo cada detalle, y los materiales de construcción, así como gran parte del mobiliario, proceden de Florencia. La terraza, con una pequeña piscina de granito de estética oriental, tiene fantásticas vistas del "sky line" del barrio.

☐ Questo spettacolare loft si trova a Tribeca, uno dei quartieri più di moda, per trovarsi all'avanguardia culturale. Oriente ed occidente si fondono in questa casa con eleganza e stile, perché abbina il gusto per l'estetica minimalista ed una collezione d'antichità asiatiche. I mobili sono minimi e in perfetta armonia con la collezione d'arte, che sposa statue di Budda con una tela di Chagall. Lo spazio originale è stato modificato, con la massima cura del minimo dettaglio. I materiali di costruzione, come gran parte dei mobili, vengono da Firenze. La terrazza, dotata di una piccola piscina di granito d'estetica orientale, vanta fantastiche viste dello "sky line" del quartiere.

Location: **New York, United States**
Architect: **Prima Design**
Photograph © **Giorgio Baroni**

Feature space: **Zen pool**

A small indoor pond in the center of the loft creates a Zen atmosphere by virtue of the water reflections. The warmth of the wooden floors, the touch of color provided by the flowers and the Italian stucco walls provide this comfortable and balanced ambiance with great liveliness.

Das kleine Wasserbecken mit den Lichtreflexen im zentralen Bereich des Lofts zeugt vom Einfluss des Zen-Buddhismus. Die warmen Töne des hölzernen Fußbodens, die Farben der Blumen und die Wände in italienischem Stuck schaffen eine ausgeglichene Atmosphäre.

Un petit étang intérieur, au centre du loft central, crée une atmosphère zen grâce aux reflets de l'eau. La qualité du parquet, les notes colorées des fleurs et les murs de stuc italien donnent vie à une ambiance confortable et harmonieuse.

Un pequeño estanque interior, que ocupa el espacio central del loft, crea una atmósfera zen mediante los reflejos del agua. La calidez de la madera del suelo, las notas de color de las flores y las paredes de estuco italiano dan vida a un ambiente confortable y equilibrado.

Un piccolo laghetto interno, che occupa lo spazio centrale del loft, crea un'atmosfera zen grazie ai riflessi dell'acqua. Il calore del legno del pavimento, le note del colore dei fiori e le pareti in stucco italiano danno vita ad un ambiente confortevole ed equilibrato.

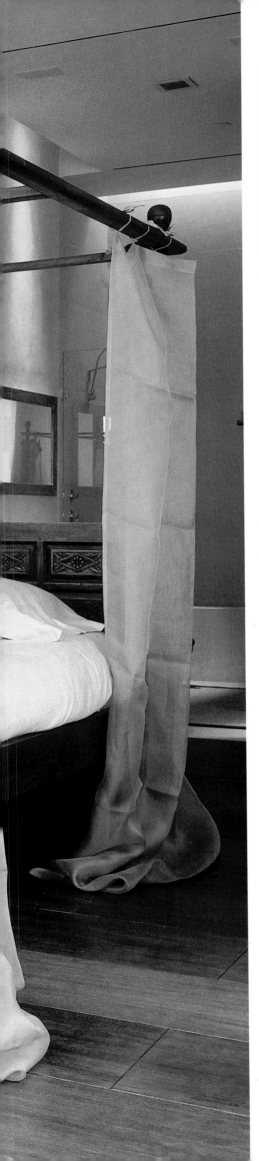

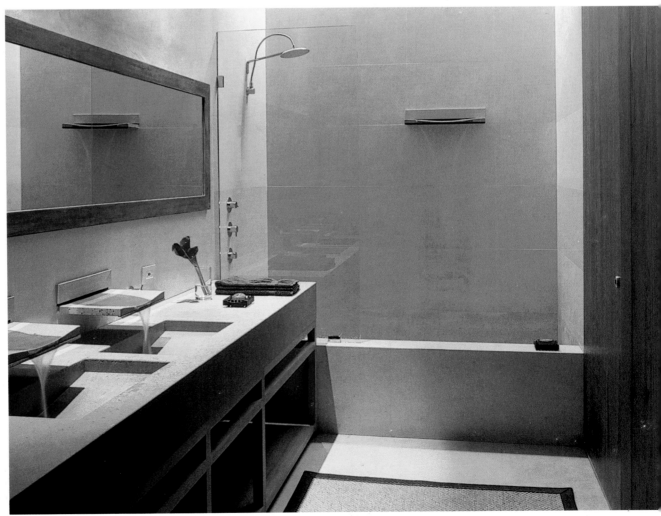

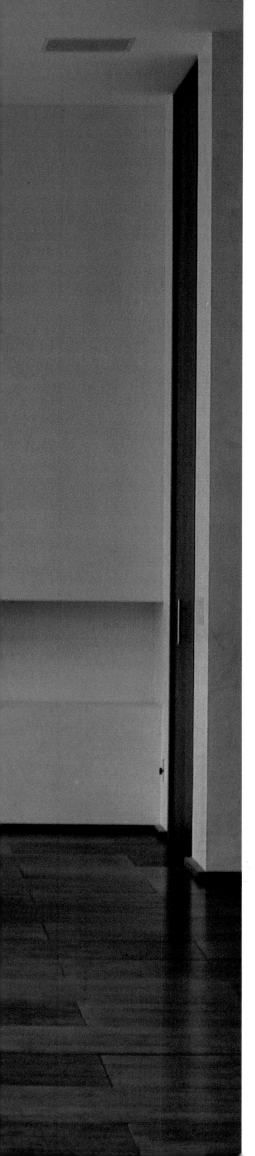

The traditional layout of a New York loft features a wide open space around which the main rooms are arranged: the living room, the living room and the kitchen. Only the bedrooms and the bathrooms are entirely private.

Typisch für die New Yorker Lofts ist der weitläufige offene Bereich, in dem sich einige der wichtigsten Aktivitäten abspielen: Wohnen, Kochen und Essen. Nur die Schlafzimmer und die Bäder sind private Räume.

Selon la distribution type du loft new-yorkais, une grande zone ouverte réunit certaines pièces principales, à l'instar du salon, de la salle à manger et de la cuisine : seules les chambres à coucher et les salles de bains sont des pièces privées.

Siguiendo la distribución típica del loft neoyorkino, una gran zona abierta reúne algunas de las estancias principales, como el salón, el comedor y la cocina; tan sólo los dormitorios y baños son estancias privadas.

Seguendo la distribuzione tipica del loft newyorkino, una grande zona aperta riunisce alcuni degli ambienti principali, come il salone, la sala da pranzo e la cucina; solo le camere da letto ed i bagni sono ambienti privati.

179

Modernity in Rio de Janeiro

☐ The impressive view of the Atlantic Ocean is not the only outstanding element of this magnificent residence. Architects created a smartly proportionate house and used bright white for its steel columns and terraces. The sliding and revolving glass panels used as walls and rooftops let the light flow into every corner of the house in perfect harmony with the tropical weather of Brazil. Air-conditioning is rendered unnecessary thanks to the sea breeze. The modern furniture features some pieces by Le Corbusier and Marcel Breuer, which emphasize the elegance and modern look of the design of this building.

☐ Die eindrucksvolle Aussicht auf den Atlantik ist nur eines der vielen herausragenden Merkmale dieses wunderbaren, leuchtend weißen Hauses mit seinen Stahlstützen und Terrassen, das von den Architekten in eleganten Proportionen entworfen wurde. Wände und Decken sind durch bewegliche, drehbare Glasscheiben ersetzt. Auf diese Weise dringt das Tageslicht in alle Winkel, und trotz des tropischen brasilianischen Klimas ist dank der frischen Brise vom Meer keine Klimaanlage erforderlich. Die moderne Eleganz des Hauses wird durch die Möbel von Le Corbusier und Marcel Breuer unterstrichen.

☐ Les impressionnantes vues sur l'océan Atlantique n'est pas le seul élément remarquable de cette magnifique résidence. Les architectes ont créé une maison d'un blanc lumineux, tant sur les colonnes d'acier que sur les terrasses, aux proportions élégantes. Les cloisons de verre, qui remplacent murs et plafonds, peuvent pivoter et coulisser, pour laisser pénétrer la lumière dans tous les coins, en parfaite harmonie avec le climat tropical brésilien et la brise de l'océan qui remplace l'air conditionné. Le mobilier moderne, doté d'œuvres de Le Corbusier et Marcel Breuer, exalte l'élégance et la modernité de l'architecture.

☐ Las impresionantes vistas al océano Atlántico no es el único elemento destacado de esta magnífica residencia; los arquitectos han creado una casa de un blanco brillante, tanto en las columnas de acero como en las terrazas, y elegantemente proporcionada. Los paneles de cristal, que sustituyen paredes y techos, pueden girar y deslizarse, con lo que la luz penetra en todos los rincones, en perfecta armonía con el clima tropical brasileño, y la brisa del océano hace innecesario el aire acondicionado. Mobiliario moderno, con piezas de Le Corbusier y Marcel Breuer, acentúan la elegancia y la modernidad de la arquitectura.

☐ Le impressionanti viste sull'oceano Atlantico non sono l'unico elemento di rilievo di questa magnifica proprietà; gli architetti hanno creato una casa di un bianco brillante, tanto nelle colonne d'acciaio come nelle terrazze, con proporzioni eleganti. I pannelli di vetro, che sostituiscono pareti e tetto, possono girare e scivolare, consentendo alla luce di penetrare in tutti gli angoli, in perfetta armonia con il clima tropicale brasiliano, e la brezza dell'oceano rende superflua l'aria condizionata. Mobili moderni, con pezzi di Le Corbusier e Marcel Breuer, accentuano l'eleganza e la modernità dell'architettura.

Location: **Rio de Janeiro, Brazil**
Architects: **Claudio Bernardes and Paulo Jacobsen**
Photograph © **Agi Simões / Zapaimages**

Feature space: **Outer terraces**

The partially covered porches and terraces that surround the house were designed to allow for enjoyment of the landscape and outdoor life. Likewise, Brazilian beige marble was used for the pavement in order to avoid landscape disruption.

Rund um das Haus wurden Loggien und halbüberdachte Terrassen eingerichtet, um beim Leben unter freiem Himmel die Umgebung genießen zu können. Der Fußboden aus sandfarbenem brasilianischen Granit harmoniert mit der Natur.

Les atriums et terrasses semi-couverts, entourant la maison, ont été conçus pour pouvoir profiter de l'environnement et vivre à l'extérieur. De même, pour ne pas briser le profil du terrain, le sol est recouvert d'un carrelage en marbre brésilien, de couleur beige.

Los porches y terrazas semicubiertas alrededor de la casa se diseñaron para poder disfrutar del entorno y hacer vida en el exterior. Asimismo, para no romper el perfil del terreno, se empleó un pavimento de mármol brasileño de color beige.

I porticati e le terrazze semicoperte intorno alla casa sono stati disegnati per godersi la natura e per vivere fuori. Inoltre, per non rompere con il paesaggio, è stato usato un pavimento di marmo brasiliano di color beige.

The house has very few partitions, with the different levels and rooms being visually and physically interconnected. The house is conceived to let in both the natural light and the breeze while the space layout and the profusely used columns give the building a lofty air.

Das Haus ist sehr offen angelegt, die unterschiedlichen Ebenen und die einzelnen Wohnbereiche gehen optisch und physisch ineinander über. Die Wohnung öffnet sich Licht und Wind und hat mit ihrer lockeren Raumaufteilung und den vielen Stützen etwas von einem Loft.

L'habitation ayant peu de cloisons intérieures, les différents niveaux et pièces communiquent entre eux, visuellement et physiquement. Conçues pour laisser pénétrer la lumière et la brise, la distribution spatiale et l'omniprésence de colonnes se rapprochent davantage du loft.

La vivienda presenta muy pocas particiones; los diferentes niveles y estancias están comunicados entre ellos, visual y físicamente. La distribución de los espacios, pensada para dejar entrar la luz y la brisa, y la presencia constante de columnas parecen más propias de un loft.

La casa presenta pochissime divisioni, i vari livelli ed ambienti sono collegati tra di loro, visivamente e fisicamente. Il tutto è stato pensato per lasciar entrare la luce e la brezza, la distribuzione degli spazi e la costante presenza di colonne sembrano più proprie di un loft.

Modernity and Distinction

☐ This duplex flat in London is an example of luxury associated to modernity marked by a sophisticated and contemporary atmosphere. The stylish and minimalist furniture made of dark wood is extremely refined; the choice of decoration and furniture creates a feeling of serenity in the rooms. Overall simplicity contributes to fuse spaces, with an integrated kitchen area that also serves as a dining room. The plain design of the living room, the warm and elegant terraces and the high quality materials used in the bedroom help create a warm atmosphere. A spectacular transparent and sculpture-like staircase rises majestically to catch the eye of the visitor.

☐ Diese zweigeschossige Wohnung in London verbindet in anspruchsvoller Atmosphäre Luxus mit Modernität. Die Möbel aus dunklem Holz sind mit ihren einfachen Linien von minimalistischer Eleganz und erfüllen die schlicht eingerichteten Räumen mit Gelassenheit. Die Einfachheit der Einrichtung lässt die Definition der Räume im Unklaren; so könnte die Office-Küche auch ein Esszimmer sein. Die Ausstattung des Wohnzimmers folgt klaren Linien, im Schlafzimmer wird mit hochwertigen Materialien ein behagliches Ambiente erzeugt und die eleganten Terrassen laden zur Entspannung ein. Eines der auffälligsten Elemente ist die spektakuläre durchsichtige Treppe, die sich stolz wie eine Skulptur erhebt.

☐ Ce duplex londonien est un exemple de luxe assorti de modernité, où l'on trouve une ambiance contemporaine et recherchée. Le mobilier, de bois foncé et aux lignes épurées, affiche élégance et minimalisme. La décoration et le mobilier choisis marquent les pièces de sérénité. Cette simplicité fait que les espaces fusionnent, comme c'est le cas de la cuisine-office, qui pourrait aussi être une salle à manger. Le salon suit des lignes dépouillées, les terrasses sont élégantes et accueillantes et dans la chambre à coucher, les matériaux employés, de grande qualité, façonnent une ambiance chaleureuse. Un des éléments qui attire le plus l'attention, est un escalier spectaculaire, transparent qui se hisse majestueusement, à l'instar d'une sculpture.

☐ Este dúplex londinense es un ejemplo de lujo asociado a la modernidad, donde se encuentra una atmósfera contemporánea y sofisticada. El mobiliario, de madera oscura y líneas depuradas, es elegante y minimalista; la decoración y el mobiliario elegidos aportan serenidad a las estancias. Esta sencillez hace que los espacios se confundan, como ocurre con la cocina-office, que podría ser un comedor. El salón es de líneas simples, las terrazas son elegantes y acogedoras y en el dormitorio se han empleado materiales de gran calidad que crean un ambiente cálido. Uno de los elementos que más llaman la atención es una espectacular escalera transparente que se alza majestuosa como si fuera una escultura.

☐ Questo duplex londinese è un esempio di lusso associato alla modernità, con un'atmosfera contemporanea e sofisticata. I mobili, in legno scuro e linee depurate, sono eleganti e minimalisti; l'arredamento ed i mobili scelti conferiscono serenità agli ambienti. Questa semplicità consente agli ambienti di confondersi, come succede con la cucina-office, che potrebbe essere una sala da pranzo. Il salone presenta linee semplici, i terrazzi sono eleganti ed accoglienti e nella stanza da letto sono stati scelti materiali di gran qualità che creano un ambiente accogliente. Uno degli elementi che più colpiscono è una spettacolare scala che si erge maestosa come se fosse una scultura.

Location: **London, United Kingdom**
Decorator: **Candy & Candy**
Photograph © **Andreas von Einsiedel**

Feature space: **Bathroom**

The hydro massage shower and the large open bath are the centerpiece of this room. Although partitions and doors divide the room into zones, the unity of space is not disrupted. The wooden furniture is of dark tones, which contrasts with the white color used in the walls, the tub and the washbasin.

Die Massagedusche und die große freistehende Badewanne beherrschen den Raum. Obwohl die einzelnen Bereiche durch Türen oder Wände voneinander getrennt sind, bleibt die Einheit des Raumes erhalten. Das Holz des Mobiliars in seinen dunklen Farbtönen hebt sich vor dem Weiß der Wände, der Badewanne und des Waschbeckens ab.

La douche à hydro-massage et la grande baignoire sont les pièces maîtresses de la pièce. La séparation des différentes zones à l'aide de portes et de cloisons ne rompt en rien l'unité de l'espace. Le bois du mobilier, aux teintes foncées, contraste avec le blanc des murs, la baignoire et le lave-mains.

La ducha de hidromasaje y la gran bañera exenta son las dos piezas protagonistas de la estancia. A pesar de que las diferentes zonas están separadas por puertas o tabiques, no se rompe la unidad del espacio. La madera del mobiliario, de tonos oscuros, contrasta con el blanco de las paredes, la bañera y el lavamanos.

La doccia con idromassaggi e la grande vasca da bagno isolata sono i due elementi protagonisti dell'ambiente. Le varie zone sono separate da porte o tramezzi, ma senza mai rompere l'unità dello spazio. Il legno dei mobili, dai toni scuri, contrasta con il bianco delle pareti, la vasca da bagno ed il lavello.

Urban Style

☐ Although at first sight this house seems to be decorated in a traditional and classical style, the small details reveal a refined taste for oriental culture: tapestries with Japanese calligraphy, bamboo chairs and some paintings and lamps reflect the owner's interest in this culture. Interiors are decorated in accordance with contemporary tastes with preference for relaxed and balanced atmospheres. The bedrooms feature magnificent large windows and neutral colors are put together on the walls to achieve an air of simplicity and extreme elegance at the same time. Its warm and distinguished living room is the perfect place to hold enjoyable evening parties.

☐ Auf den ersten Blick scheint diese Wohnung im traditionellen, klassischen Stil eingerichtet worden zu sein, doch kleine Details offenbaren eine Vorliebe für Asien: Bezugsstoffe mit japanischen Schriftzeichen, Bambusstühle, Bilder und Lampen zeugen vom Interesse für Fernost. Die Innenräume sind nach zeitgenössischen Vorstellungen dekoriert und vermitteln Ruhe und Ausgewogenheit. Die Schlafräume mit ihren großzügigen Fenstern sind mit ihrer neutralen Farbgebung schlicht und elegant gehalten. Der behagliche, vornehme Salon ist ein beliebter Ort für Abendgesellschaften und angeregte Unterhaltung.

☐ A première vue cette demeure semble offrir un décor de style classique et traditionnel. Toutefois, des petits détails révèlent un goût raffiné pour la culture orientale : tapisseries dotées d'écriture japonaise, fauteuils de bambou et autres cadres et lampes reflètent l'engouement de la propriétaire pour cette culture. Les intérieurs sont décorés dans le goût contemporain marquant la préférence pour les atmosphères paisibles et harmonieuses. Les chambres à coucher, aux majestueuses baies vitrées, sont dotées d'une simplicité apparente et d'une élégance extrême, nées du mélange de couleurs neutres. Le salon, accueillant et distingué, est un lieu très séduisant où passer d'agréables veillées.

☐ A primera vista esta vivienda parece haber sido decorada con un estilo clásico y tradicional; sin embargo, los pequeños detalles revelan un gusto refinado por la cultura oriental: tapicerías con escritura japonesa, butacas de bambú y algunos cuadros y lámparas reflejan el interés del propietario por esta cultura. Los interiores están decorados según el gusto contemporáneo y se ha optado por atmósferas tranquilas y equilibradas. Los dormitorios, con majestuosos ventanales, aparecen simples y extremamente elegantes al combinar colores de gama neutra. El salón, acogedor y distinguido, es un lugar de gran atractivo donde pasar agradables veladas.

☐ A prima vista questa casa sembra essere stata arredata in stile classico e tradizionale; ma, i piccoli dettagli rivelano un raffinato gusto per la cultura orientale: la tappezzeria con scrittura giapponese, le poltrone in bambù ed alcuni quadri e lampade riflettono l'interesse del proprietario per questa cultura. Gli interni sono arredati in stile contemporaneo avendo scelto atmosfere tranquille ed equilibrate. Le stanze da letto, con i loro maestosi finestroni, appaiono semplici ed estremamente eleganti per la gamma dei colori neutri usati. Il salone, accogliente ed elegante, è un luogo di grande bellezza in cui trascorrere gradevoli serate.

Location: **London, United Kingdom**
Architect: **Candy & Candy**
Photograph © **Andreas von Einsiedel**

Feature space: **Dining room**

The dining room is a modern and stylish room that brings together traditional and contemporary elements. The crystal candelabra and the moldings of the ceiling lend the room a classical air, which is in contrast with the contemporary painting placed over the fireplace.

Im eleganten Esszimmer treffen traditionelle und moderne Elemente aufeinander. Die Lüster und die Stuckverzierungen der Decke stehen für eine klassische Auffassung, die mit dem Gemälde eines zeitgenössischen Künstlers über dem Kamin lebhaft kontrastiert.

La salle à manger est une pièce élégante et moderne qui conjugue éléments traditionnels et contemporains. Les lustres de cristal et les moulures des plafonds confèrent un air classique qui contraste avec le tableau d'art contemporain accroché au-dessus de la cheminée.

El comedor es una estancia elegante y moderna que reúne elementos tradicionales con otros contemporáneos. Los candelabros de cristal y las molduras de los techos aportan un aire clásico que contrasta con el cuadro de arte contemporáneo situado sobre la chimenea.

La sala da pranzo è un ambiente elegante e moderno con elementi tradizionali abbinati ad altri contemporanei. I candelabri di cristallo e le modanature del tetto conferiscono un'aria classica che contrasta con il quadro d'arte contemporanea posto sul camino.

The large windows enhance the decoration of the bedrooms by ensuring an abundant flow of daylight that helps create a feeling of amplitude, thus achieving a refined and elegant ambiance.

Die großflächigen Fenster tragen zur Großzügigkeit der Schlafräume bei; das reichlich einfallende natürliche Licht verstärkt das Gefühl der Weite und es entstehen raffinierte, distinguierte Gemächer.

Les baies vitrées enrichissent la décoration des chambres à coucher : très grandes, elles tamisent la lumière naturelle abondante en accroissant la sensation d'espace, créant des univers élégants et raffinés.

Los ventanales enriquecen la decoración de los dormitorios: de grandes dimensiones, abastecen de luz natural abundante y aumentan la sensación de amplitud, lo que crea unos ambientes elegantes y refinados.

I finestroni arricchiscono l'arredamento delle stanze da letto: di grandi dimensioni, lasciano passare abbondante luce naturale, aumentando la sensazione di spazio, creando dunque degli ambienti eleganti e raffinati.

Fusion of Two Periods

☐ This London house is characterized for the simplicity of its decoration without overlooking the elegance that is emphasized by the great dimensions of the building. High ceilings and large windows help create a luminous and clear ambiance. Some pieces of furniture stand on their own by virtue of their singularity and quality. A unique fusion of tradition and modernity is achieved by combining some classical furniture such as the two antique chairs placed at the study table. The different styles enhance and emphasize the rich interiors and the singularity of the main bedroom by using an outer wooden top and a circular window, two of this house's distinguishing features.

☐ Diese Wohnung in London zeichnet sich durch die schlichte, aber distinguierte Dekoration der großzügigen Räumlichkeiten aus. Hohe Decken und große Fenster schaffen helle Räume, in denen die ausgesuchten Möbelstücke hervorragend zur Geltung kommen. Durch die Kombination klassischer Stücke, etwa der beiden antiken Stühle beim Schreibtisch, wird eine einzigartige Verschmelzung von Tradition und Moderne erreicht. Die unterschiedlichen Stile unterstreichen ihrerseits die Eigenart der Räume. Das Schlafzimmer mit seiner Holzdecke und dem runden Fenster steht exemplarisch für den unverwechselbaren Charakter des Hauses.

☐ Le dépouillement de la décoration qui ne manque pas d'élégance, associée aux grandes dimensions de la maison sont deux caractéristiques qui définissent cette demeure londonienne. Plafonds hauts et baies vitrées créent des ambiances claires et lumineuses. La qualité et l'originalité des pièces de mobilier en font des pièces uniques. Le mélange de meubles classiques, comme les deux chaises anciennes aux côtés de la table du studio, crée une fusion extraordinaire entre tradition et modernisme. Les différents styles exaltent et mettent en valeur des intérieurs riches, et l'originalité de la chambre à coucher des maîtres, avec son plafond boisé et sa baie vitrée circulaire, est un exemple de l'unicité de la demeure.

☐ La sencillez en la decoración, no exenta de elegancia, junto con las grandes dimensiones de la casa son dos de los rasgos que definen esta vivienda de Londres. Techos altos y ventanales crean ambientes claros y luminosos; las piezas del mobiliario destacan por sí solas gracias a su calidad y singularidad. La combinación de muebles clásicos, como las dos sillas antiguas junto a la mesa del estudio, consigue una fantástica fusión de tradición y modernidad. Los diferentes estilos realzan y potencian unos interiores ricos y el singular dormitorio principal, con el techo de madera y un ventanal circular, es un ejemplo del inconfundible carácter de la vivienda.

☐ La semplicità nell'arredamento, non esente d'eleganza, insieme alle grandi dimensioni della casa sono due delle caratteristiche che definiscono questa casa di Londra. Tetti alti e finestroni creano ambienti chiari e luminosi; i vari mobili spiccano da per sé grazie alla loro qualità e singolarità. L'abbinamento di mobili classici, come le due sedie antiche vicino al tavolo dello studio, offre una fantastica fusione di tradizione e modernità. I vari stili mettono in evidenza e rafforzano degli interni ricchi e la singolare stanza da letto principale, dotata di un soffitto di legno ed una finestra tonda, è un esempio del carattere inconfondibile della casa.

Location: **London, United Kingdom**
Architects: **Julian Powell-Tuck (renovation), CR Ashbee (original building)**
Photograph © **Andreas von Einsiedel**

Feature space: **Living room**

Contemporary art works of great size are displayed on the walls of the living room. Comfort and warmth are ensured along with a modern ambiance in this large room that features a wooden floor and a generous flow of natural light.

Die Wände des Wohnzimmers sind mit großformatigen Werken zeitgenössischer Künstler geschmückt. Trotz seiner Größe und der modernen Einrichtung ist ein komfortabler Raum entstanden, dem die Holzfußböden und das einfallende Tageslicht Behaglichkeit verleihen.

Les murs du salon exhibent des œuvres d'art contemporain de grand format. La modernité de l'ambiance et la générosité de l'espace n'ôtent ni qualité, ni chaleur, à la salle, ceci en grande partie grâce aux parquets et à l'entrée de la lumière naturelle.

En las paredes del salón se exhiben obras de arte contemporáneo de gran formato. La modernidad del ambiente y la amplitud del espacio no restan comodidad ni calidez a la sala, gracias en gran parte a los suelos de madera y la entrada de luz natural.

Sulle pareti del salone sono esposte opere d'arte contemporanee di gran formato. La modernità dell'ambiente e la grandezza dello spazio non alterano la comodità ed il calore della sala, in gran misura grazie ai pavimenti di legno e la luce naturale che vi entra.

The fusion of modernity and tradition that can be seen throughout the house enhances the interiors and allows for the enjoyment of excellent works of art and furniture of different periods, as is the case with the exquisite antique chairs upholstered in embossed leather placed by the study table.

Die Verschmelzung von Moderne und Tradition ist in der gesamten Wohnung spürbar. Sie bereichert die Innenausstattung und dank ihr sind hervorragende Kunstwerke und Möbelstücke verschiedener Stilepochen zu bewundern, wie die beiden lederbespannten Stühle neben dem Schreibtisch.

La fusion entre modernité et tradition est présente dans toute l'habitation, enrichissant l'intérieur tout en permettant de profiter des merveilleuses œuvres d'art et du mobilier d'époques différentes, à l'instar de ces ravissants fauteuils anciens, recouverts de cuir travaillé, placés juste côté de la table du studio.

La fusión de modernidad y tradición está presente en toda la vivienda, enriquece el interior y permite disfrutar de excelentes obras de arte y mobiliario de varias épocas, como es el caso de estas exquisitas sillas antiguas tapizadas con cuero trabajado que se hallan junto a la mesa del estudio.

La fusione della modernità e della tradizione è presente in tutta la casa, arricchisce l'interno e consente di godersi eccellenti opere d'arte e mobili di varie epoche, come nel caso di queste squisite sedie antiche tappezzate in cuoio lavorato che si trovano accanto al tavolo dello studio.

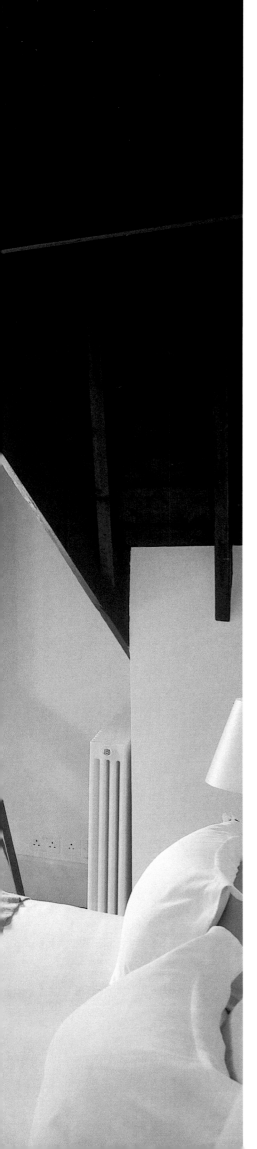

Schur Residence

☐ This modern 8.073-square-feet building is located in a wealthy neighborhood of Palm Beach. The only special requirement made by the owner was that the building should be modern and spectacular. Two slim volumes rising perpendicularly from the main plane and a two storey space connecting both wings are the entrance to the living room and the dining room. Interiors are made up of wide spaces; vertical surfaces refract the sunlight and create a soft illumination. Likewise, various works of art by contemporary artists emphasize the luxury and exclusivity of the house also conveyed by its architectural design.

☐ Dieses moderne, 750 m² große Haus liegt in einem wohlhabenden Wohnviertel von Palm Beach. Der Bauherr stellte keine besonderen Ansprüche außer dem Wunsch, ein aufsehenerregendes modernes Wohnhaus sein eigen nennen zu können. Auf den ersten Blick fallen die beiden schlanken senkrechten Baukörper auf, die über einen zweigeschossigen Bau miteinander verbunden sind. Dieser Mittelbau zwischen den beiden Flügeln stellt den Zugang zum Wohnzimmer und zum Esszimmer dar. Die Innenräume sind sehr weitläufig, die vertikalen Flächen werfen das Licht zurück und es entsteht eine angenehme Beleuchtung. Die Werke zeitgenössischer Künstler unterstreichen den exklusiven Luxus der Architektur des Hauses.

☐ Cette construction moderne de 750 m² est située dans un voisinage cossu de Palm Beach. Le programme, libre de toute contrainte particulière, devait uniquement répondre au désir du propriétaire de créer une architecture moderne et spectaculaire. Le regard est attiré par la sveltesse des deux volumes perpendiculaires du premier plan, et par un espace à double hauteur qui connecte ces deux ailes et sert d'entrée au salon et à la salle à manger. L'intérieur se compose d'espaces généreux. Les superficies verticales réfléchissent la lumière et créent un doux éclairage. En outre, diverses œuvres d'artistes contemporains accentuent le luxe et l'exclusivité de la demeure, transmis par l'architecture.

☐ Esta moderna construcción de 750 m² está situada en un acomodado vecindario de Palm Beach. No hubo ningún requerimiento especial en el programa, excepto el deseo del propietario de crear una arquitectura moderna y espectacular. Destacan dos esbeltos volúmenes perpendiculares al plano primario y un espacio de doble altura que conecta estas dos alas y actúa como entrada al salón y al comedor. El interior se compone de espacios amplios; las superficies verticales refractan la luz y crean una suave iluminación. Asimismo, varias obras de artistas contemporáneos acentúan el lujo y la exclusividad de la vivienda que ya transmite la arquitectura.

☐ Questa moderna costruzione di 750 m² si trova in un quartiere residenziale di Palm Beach. Nel programma non c'è stata nessuna richiesta speciale, salvo il desiderio del proprietario di creare un'architettura moderna e spettacolare. Spiccano due slanciati volumi perpendicolari al piano di base ed uno spazio di doppia altezza che collega queste due ali, e che funge da ingresso al salone ed alla sala da pranzo. L'interno è composto di grandi spazi; le superfici verticali riflettono la luce creando un'illuminazione soft. Inoltre, varie opere d'artisti contemporanei accentuano il lusso e l'unicità della casa che già da per sé trasmette l'architettura.

Location: **Palm Beach, Florida, United States**
Architect: **Mojo Stumer Associates, p.c.**
Photograph © **Scott Francis, Phill Ennis**

Feature space: **Transit areas**

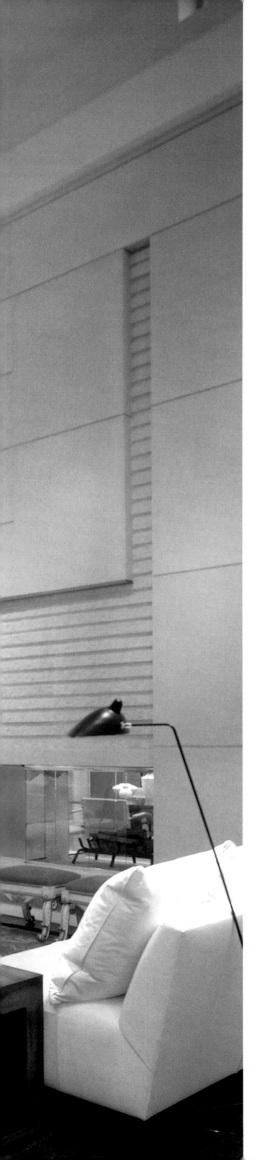

The living room brings together different areas within a single space. The stairway connects the different levels of the house and is located in a glass case that allow for the enjoyment of both inside and outside views.

Das Wohnzimmer vereint verschiedene Bereiche. Die Treppe verbindet die verschiedenen Ebenen des Hauses. Sie ist in einem verglasten Baukörper untergebracht, sodass man einen wunderbaren Ausblick nach drinnen und draußen genießt.

Le salon réunit diverses zones en un même espace. L'escalier connecte les différents niveaux de la demeure, inséré dans un espace tout en verre, permettant de profiter à la fois des vues intérieures et extérieures.

El salón reúne diversas áreas en una misma estancia. La escalera conecta los diferentes niveles de la vivienda y se halla en un espacio acristalado, lo que permite disfrutar de las vistas exteriores e interiores.

Il salone riunisce varie zone in un unico ambiente. La scala collega i vari livelli della casa e si trova in uno spazio vetrato, che consente di godersi le viste esterne e gli interni.

Luminosity and fluency are the main features of the transit zones that connect the different areas in the house. An impressive six-meter tall glass window allows a full view of the two wings of the house and gives a majestic quality to the interior.

Die Übergangsbereiche verbinden die verschiedenen Teile des Hauses und zeichnen sich durch ihre Helligkeit aus. Eine eindrucksvolle, sechs Meter hohe Glaswand vermittelt eine klare Vorstellung von den beiden Flügeln des Hauses und seinem großzügigen Inneren.

Les zones de passage reliant les différentes sphères de la maison, fascinent par leur luminosité et fluidité. Un impressionnant mur de verre de six mètres de haut permet de percevoir clairement les deux ailes, tout en conférant à l'intérieur une allure majestueuse.

Las zonas de paso que conectan las distintas áreas de la casa destacan por su luminosidad y fluidez. Una impresionante pared de cristal de seis metros de altura permite tener una percepción clara de las dos alas y proporciona majestuosidad al interior.

Le zone di passaggio che collegano le varie parti della casa spiccano per la loro luminosità e fluidità. Un'impressionante parete di vetro di sei metri d'altezza consente di avere una chiara percezione delle due ali, conferendo maestosità agli interni.

A spacious dining room is located next to one of the large glass windows; the luminous room features a large contemporary painting that enhances the modern aspect of its furniture.

Gleich neben einer der Glaswände liegt ein großes, lichtdurchflutetes Esszimmer mit modernen Möbeln, das von einem großformatigen, zeitgenössischen Gemälde beherrscht wird.

Attenante à un des grands murs de verre, on trouve la salle à manger, inondée de lumière et présidée par une grande toile d'art contemporain qui exalte le modernisme du mobilier.

Junto a una de las grandes paredes de cristal, se halla un amplio comedor, inundado de luz y presidido por un gran lienzo de arte contemporáneo, que acentúa la modernidad del mobiliario.

Vicino ad una delle grandi pareti in vetro, vi è una grande sala da pranzo, inondata dalla luce e presieduta da una grande tela d'arte contemporanea, che accentua la modernità dell'arredamento.